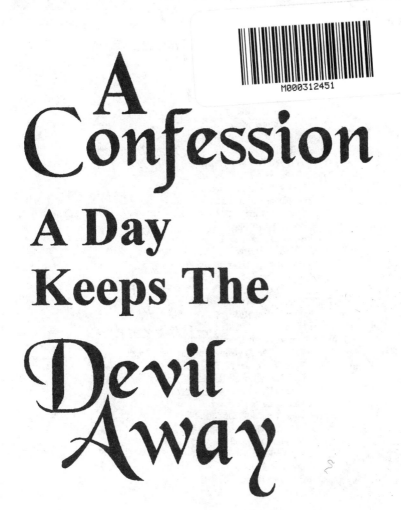

A Confession
A Day
Keeps The
Devil Away

Frances Hunter

Published By
Charles and Frances Hunter
Po Box 5600 * Kingwood, Texas 77325-5600
(281) 358-7575 * 1-800-683-3024
Email: wec@cfhunter.org * www.cfhunter.org

Books By Charles ❧ Frances Hunter

A Confession A Day Keeps The Devil Away
Angels On Assignment
Are You Tired?
Born Again! What Do You Mean?
Come Alive
Follow Me
Go, Man, Go
God Is Fabulous
God's Answer To Fat...Loøse It!
God's Conditions For Prosperity
Handbook For Healing
Hang Loose With Jesus
Healing
Heart To Heart Flip Chart
His Power Through You
Holy Laughter
Hot Line To Heaven
How Do You Treat My Son Jesus?
How To Heal The Sick
How To Make Your Marriage Exciting
How To Pick A Perfect Husband...Or Wife
How To Overcome "Cool Down" & Keep The Fire Burning
How To Receive & Maintain A Healing
How To Receive & Minister The Baptism With The Holy Spirit
I Don't Follow Signs & Wonders...They Follow Me
If You Really Love Me...
Impossible Miracles
Memorizing Made Easy
Possessing The Mind Of Christ
P.T.L.A. (Praise The Lord Anyway)
Since Jesus Passed By
the fabulous Skinnie Minnie Recipe Book
Strength For Today
Supernatural Horizons (From Glory To Glory)
The Two Sides Of A Coin
This Way Up
Video Study Guide-How To Heal The Sick (15 Hours)
Video Study Guide-How To Heal The Sick Power Pack (6 Hours)
Why Should "I" Speak In Tongues?

ISBN 0-917726-37-5
©Copyright 1980 by Charles and Frances Hunter, all rights reserved.
ISBN 1-878209-13-2
©Copyright 1995 by Charles and Frances Hunter, all rights reserved.
Scripture quotations are taken from:
The New King James Version (NKJ) ©1979, 1980, 1982 by Thomas Nelson, Inc., Nashville, TN.
The Authorized King James Version (KJV)
The Living Bible, Paraphrased (TLB) ©1971 by Tyndale House Publishers, Wheaton, IL.
The Amplified New Testament (AMP) ©1954, 1958 by The Lockman Foundation.
The Holy Bible, New International Version (NIV) ©1978 by New York International Bible Society,
published by Zondervan Bible Publishers, Grand Rapids, MI.
All references not specified are taken from the New King James Version.

CONTENTS

Introduction

"Anyone who wants to follow me must put aside his own desires and conveniences and carry his cross with him every day and KEEP CLOSE TO ME!" (Luke 9:23 TLB).

"When he arrived and saw the wonderful things God was doing he was filled with excitement and joy, and encouraged the believers to stay CLOSE TO THE LORD, whatever the cost" (Acts 11:23 TLB).

"And when you draw close to God, God will draw close to you...let your hearts be filled with God alone to make them pure and true to him" (James 4:8 TLB).

Inside of every born again believer, there is an insatiable hunger to draw close and then closer to God. There is only one way to accomplish this heavenly desire within us, and that is to read the Word of God, meditate on it, and then speak it at all times!

There is a constant need within each and every one of our own lives to hear and speak the Word of God and have our faith renewed by discovering afresh and anew His wonderful promises for each and every one of us.

Where do you start, and where do you end? We've chosen different subjects to confess each month — THE WORD; FAITH; PROSPERITY; THE NAME OF JESUS; BLESSINGS; LOVE; FREEDOM FROM FEAR; GENERAL; HEALING; HOLY SPIRIT; PRAISE; AND SALVATION!

What do you do when it's the month of March where we confess prosperity, and your need is to be delivered from fear? Jump over to the scriptures and confessions on fear, and don't worry about getting out-of-date or out-of-order!

Put this book where you can see it at all times and read over some of these daily devotions more than once, and see what happens to you. Read each day's devotion several times during the day until the Word of God sticks to your ribs, or gets into your heart! When you make your devotion for the day, read the scripture first each time. Read it out loud so you can hear it–

"So then faith comes by hearing, and hearing by the word of God" *(Romans 10:17).* You might even want to get your Bible out and read several verses before and after so that the whole meaning of the scripture and the resulting devotion will come alive in your spirit!

On trips, as we ride along between cities, in a car or on planes, one of us reads the scripture, followed by the daily devotion. After that we discuss it, and it's amazing the light we receive just by this simple process. Try it! Unsaved mates have been known to be reached through this simple message as they gave their explanation of what they thought the Word said! Some months we even read ALL the devotions every day!

It's an extra blessing to see family unity strengthened by confessing and reading God's Word together. Fussing, complaining and arguing turns to praising and loving God, and each other, IN JESUS' NAME!

This is one of the most powerful things which has ever happened in our lives – let it happen in yours!

It takes time to read the scriptures and memorize them, but the time you spend will be the most valuable time you have ever spent!

Special Note From Charles Hunter:

As I carefully re-read this daily confession book, my spirit soared because the amazing love of God came forth with such power and truth. By reading the entire book through as a "book" instead of a daily confession, the keen desire in my heart to "Draw Closer to God and to Jesus" became a reality. This can happen to you, too! Frances has done such a marvelous job of selecting just the right scriptures to inspire you into a higher plane of love for God and Jesus, and her confessions make them so real you feel that you have just walked through the veil split by God as Jesus made a way to go directly into the throne room and be in the very presence of God.

Try reading the whole book through; then as the Spirit quickens you, read a whole month at one sitting; but don't fail to read the daily confessions!

Charles

THE WORD

"In the beginning God created the heavens and the earth" *(Genesis 1:1).*

God took nothing and from nothing He created the universe.

How did He create it? From Hebrews 11:3 we get the important clue which can unlock the entire Bible to you in a totally new and different way: *"By faith we understand that the worlds were framed by the word of God, so that the things which are seen were not made of things which are visible."*

By the WORD of God. Not by the hands of God. Not by the feet of God. Not by the mind of God. Not by the Power of God, but BY THE WORD OF GOD.

We can create a whole new world for ourselves by speaking the WORD of God for our lives!

It's one thing to read the Word of God, it's another thing to memorize the Word of God, but when you possess it, what you're saying is, it's mine, it's mine, it's mine! I take it for myself!

Jan. 1   *"For the word of God is living and powerful, and sharper than any two-edged sword, piercing even to the division of soul and spirit, and of joints and marrow, and is a discerner of the thoughts and intents of the heart." Hebrews 4:12*

Glory, Father, nothing can withstand the sword of your Word, which is mightier and more forceful than all the nuclear power in this world! With that sword in my hand each and every day, there's nothing I can't overcome! I'm a winner, not a loser, because your Word has made it so. I delight and revel in the power of your wonderful Word, which cleanses my heart, lifts my thoughts heavenward and is like an invincible two-edged sword preparing the way before me! It's quick, too, because it doesn't take long to hit the target!

Jan. 2   *"For 'Who has known the mind of the Lord that he may instruct Him?' But we have the mind of Christ."*
I Corinthians 2:16

Father, what a privilege to know that I'm not operating with a natural mind. I praise you that my thoughts are heavenly because I have the mind of Christ! I thank you that I don't have to worry about those silly things that come into my mind every once in a while, because when they start, I can just relax and realize that I have the mind of Christ. I don't have to hang onto the garbage and worries of the world, but instead I'm concentrating on my eternal destination, and I thank you and praise you for that!

Jan. 3   *"So shall My word be that goes forth from My mouth; it shall not return to Me void, but it shall accomplish what I please, and it shall prosper in the thing for which I sent it." Isaiah 55:11*

Father, I thank you that your Word does everything, and all that you say it will do. I thank you that it accomplishes exactly what you say, without any "if's," "and's" or "but's." I thank you for the knowledge that nothing your Word says shall ever fall by the wayside and die. I praise you because you've said it never returns to you void. I bless you, Father, that your Word grows, multiplies, thrives, flourishes, blossoms and blooms wherever and whenever you send it. I praise you that it never dies on the vine, but is constantly growing and multiplying!

Jan. 4   *"...blessed are those who hear the word of God and keep it!" Luke 11:28*

Father, I bless you because I am blessed! I have heard your Word and I keep it hidden in my heart that I might not sin against you. I thank you that because I keep your Word, I am blessed in everything I do. I thank you because I have had the opportunity to hear your Word. Father, I am blessed among all the people of every nation in the world because I have the opening at all times to hear your Word. I thank you for a Word which permeates my entire being, and blesses me as I read it, memorize it, and confess it! Father, I am keeping it in my heart forever, and I love you for giving your Word!

Jan. 5   *"All Scripture is given by inspiration of God, and is profitable for doctrine, for reproof, for correction, for instruction in righteousness." II Timothy 3:16*

Father, I praise you that there is no guesswork with scripture. I thank you for the knowledge that every single word has been given by inspiration of God. I thank you that you had many purposes in inspiring those men of old to write down your thoughts, because it establishes doctrine, creed and dogma for us. I praise you, Father, that your Word has power to rebuke, admonish and censure us. I bless you that when I get out of line, your Word is right there to correct me and get me straightened out again, but most of all, Father, I bless you for giving me instructions on how to live in the beauty of your righteousness! Glory, I'm walking in righteousness!

Jan. 6   *"Heaven and earth will pass away, but My words will by no means pass away." Mark 13:31*

Father, how I praise you because the things of this world are transient -- friends are transient, possessions are subject to change, but your Word is not! I bless you that even though everything else goes down the drain, your words shall remain forever and forever. Thank you, Father, that we come into this world in a perishable container which we know won't last forever, but you have given us something to put into that temporary housing that will last eternally, and that is your Word! Bless you, Father, that even when the storms of life are thundering all around us and it looks as though everything may fall apart, that I can stand on the secure knowledge that your words shall never pass away!

Jan. 7   *"But Jesus answered him, saying, 'It is written, "Man shall not live by bread alone, but by every word of God."'" Luke 4:4*

I praise you, Father, for the spiritual banquet you've given me in your Word. I feast every day on manna, and this body of mine thrives on the heavenly vitamins you provide. I thank you that I do not have to live by the physical things alone, but that I can find spiritual health in your Word which assures me of a healthy body, a sound mind, and an endless supply of enthusiasm for tackling the tasks you put before me each day. Father, thank you for not wasting one single word, but for making each and every word count in my life. I love you for that!

Jan. 8   *"If you abide in Me, and My words abide in you, you will ask what you desire, and it shall be done for you." John 15:7*

Father, I love that word "abide." I praise you that as long as I dwell, reside, live, stay in and submit to you, and let your words snuggle down deep inside of me, that you have given me the awesome privilege of asking whatever I will, and then resting safe and secure in the knowledge that it will be done for me. I bless you because you simply gave me those two little conditions, that I had to abide in you, and let your words abide in me, for those blessings of Abraham to overtake and overcome me. Bless you, Father, for not being a stingy God and promising us only one thing for abiding in you, but for promising us everything!

Jan. 9   *"...I am ready to perform My word." Jer. 1:12*

Father, I bless you that you lose no time performing your Word. I can see you in my mind speeding up and expediting all the things you've promised, because you are not a God who sits back and does nothing but you are a God of action! I thank you that you make short work of those things which stand in the way of the performance of your Word. I thank you, Father, that you don't use delaying tactics like the devil does, but that you are prompt and right on schedule at all times in fulfilling your Word!

Jan. 10 *"Your word I have hidden in my heart, that I might not sin against you; Forever, O Lord, your word is settled in heaven." Psalm 119:11, 89*

Father, thank you for letting me hide your wonderful, brilliant, resplendent, dazzling, glorious words in my heart for the purpose of having them there to remind me not to sin. Your words are so sharp and penetrating, they can go through the greatest temptation that might ever come my way, to protect me from the fiery darts of the devil himself. I praise you for that weapon with which to protect myself at all times from sin. And how I thank you, Father, that we have no arguing and debating about your Word, because it has been settled in heaven for all times! Not down here on earth, Father, but right up in heaven with you! Bless you, Father, that I live by heaven-made rules and don't have to depend on the peculiarities of men to live by!

Jan. 11 *"Your word is a lamp to my feet and a light to my path." Psalm 119:105*

Father, I bless you that I'm not stumbling around in the dark wondering which way to go. Bless you that you have put your Word unto my feet so that I may receive understanding and enlightenment to my mind, my heart and my soul! Father, I love your law and I meditate in it day and night because of the glorious light it sheds abroad. I thank you that the path on which I walk is one where I have no fear that I might fall down in the darkness, because it is flooded with light with no hiding places for sin to lurk and get me. Thank you that your light is brighter than any light man has ever developed, and that it's turned right onto my path!

Jan. 12 *"The entrance of your words gives light; it gives understanding to the simple." Psalm 119:130*

Father, how I thank you that your Word broke through the cold, stony heart I once had. I praise you that when one single word sneaked through that crevice in my sinful armor, it began to give light to my life. Thank you that the unfolding of your Word gave me understanding, discernment and comprehension even though my mind was simple. How I longed for your words to give me more and more light, and because of this you were merciful to me and showed me your favor, and have established my steps and directed them by means of your Word! I love your Word, so I'll keep on hearing, receiving, loving and obeying!

Jan. 13 *"The law of your mouth is better to me than thousands of shekels of gold and silver." Psalm 119:72*

Father, how I bless you that the world can have its silver and gold, with its fluctuating prices, but your Word stands above all of the treasures of this world and never changes. I praise you because your promises surpass anything this world has to offer. Thank you that it is better than silver and gold, houses and lands, or any other kind of material possessions. I thank you that the entrance of your Word illumines my entire life and that you teach me good judgment, wise and right discernment and knowledge, and that the earth is full of your loving kindness and mercy.

Jan. 14 *"Therefore whoever hears these sayings of Mine, and does them, I will liken him to a wise man who built his house on the rock: and the rain descended, the floods came, and the winds blew and beat on that house; and it did not fall, for it was founded on the rock." Matt. 7:24,25*

Father, I praise you that my house is built upon a rock because I have heard your Word, and am a doer of the Word, and not just a hearer. I bless you that because of this you have called me a wise and productive person, who is practical in his ways. I bless you, Father, for the promise of your Word which says that when the rains fell and the floods overflowed, and even when the winds became hurricane force and beat upon my house, it didn't fall because it was founded on a rock. Father, I bless you that your Word didn't allow me to be foolish and build my house upon the sand, so that when the winds came, my house blew down! I praise you that my house is standing on that solid rock!

Jan. 15 *"It is the Spirit who gives life; the flesh profits nothing. The words that I speak to you are spirit, and they are life." John 6:63*

Father, I praise you that the Spirit quickens your Word. I thank you that the Spirit is the Life-giver; because there is no profit in the flesh. I thank you that the words which you have spoken and recorded in your Word give me spirit and life. I bless you, Father, that I am not dead in the trespasses of sin and disaster, but that I am alive because my spirit has been quickened, energized and made alive by your Words!

Jan. 16 *"You are of God, little children, and have overcome them, because He who is in you is greater than he who is in the world." I John 4:4*

Father, how I applaud and glorify your Word. I thank you for the magnificent promises in your Word. I thank you, Father, that your Son, Jesus Christ, lives big in me and he is greater and mightier than the devil and all his doings. I don't have to submit to his torment any longer, because I know that I know that I know that what your Word tells me is true. You have said that there is a greater one living in me than is living in the world, and I believe it, receive it, confess it and possess this promise for myself! I thank you that regardless of how big the devil might look to me in certain situations, that I can stand tall and look down on him, knowing that I have far more power than he does!

Jan. 17   *"This Book of the Law shall not depart from your mouth, but you shall meditate in it day and night, that you may observe to do according to all that is written in it. For then you will make your way prosperous, and then you will have good success." Joshua 1:8*

Your Word is in my mouth, Father, and I'm not taking it out! For too many years I had the filth of the devil coming out, and I like what you've given me. I praise you that I am made righteous and have right standing with you because of your saving grace. I thank you that because I am doing everything according to what is written in your law, I am prospering, and having good success. I praise you, Father, that I don't have to depend on the world for instructions on how to be successful, but that I can depend on your Word, because you don't make provision for failure, you only make provision for success! I'm prospering! I'm successful! I'm blessed!–because you said so!

Jan. 18   *"There is therefore now no condemnation to those who are in Christ Jesus, who do not walk according to the flesh, but according to the Spirit." Romans 8:1*

Father, I thank you that I walk in victory today and EVERY day because I have been redeemed by the blood of the Lamb. I'm washed clean inside and out, because the best detergent in the whole world is that precious blood. Therefore, I have no condemnation or guilt in my life because my sins are washed away FOREVER! Father, I'm not interested in walking after the flesh, because that leads to death, but I'm walking after the law of the Spirit of life, which is the law of my new being, and it has freed me from the law of sin and death. Hallelujah! I'm not only walking, but I'm dancing in the newness of life!

Jan. 19 *"What then shall we say to these things? If God is for us, who can be against us?" Romans 8:31*

There's another one of your wonderful promises, Father, and I praise and glorify you because YOU ARE FOR ME! Together, you and I make a majority, and nothing and no one can stand against us. Father, by myself, I might not be so super, but with you I'm a majority at all times. I bless you that I don't have to rely on my own strength, but I'm walking in your power and might, and together we can move mountains. Hallelujah! I'm victorious because you're on my side. The devil can't win against me, his angels can't win against me, so there is no way they can successfully be against me! You could make it without me, but I sure can't do it without you!

Jan. 20 *"Therefore, if anyone is in Christ, he is a new creation; old things have passed away; behold, all things have become new." II Corinthians 5:17*

Father, I praise you that I am in Christ because I have been born again of the incorruptible seed that can't be contaminated, spoiled or tainted! I thank you that I am a NEW creature. I praise you that the individual who was me a few short years ago, no longer exists. I praise you that all of the things of my old nature have passed away, and that I'm a brand new creature in Christ. I praise you that everything about me has changed and that all things are NEW! I praise you that the month of January always ushers in a new year, and it reminds me of the newness of life in Christ Jesus. I praise you for making me and keeping me NEW!

Jan. 21 *"Do not lie to one another, since you have put off the old man with his deeds, and have put on the new man who is renewed in knowledge according to the image of Him who created him." Colossians 3:9,10*

Glory to God, I'm a new man! Father, I praise you for making the Christian life so simple, because you so beautifully tell us what to do and what not to do. Thank you that I have put off the old man with all my evil, and have put on the new man. I like the new "me" better! I thank you that my mind is renewed and is no longer conformed to this world, because I have been created in your beautiful image. I love you, Father, and praise you for loving me so much that you put all these beautiful promises in your Word!

Jan. 22 *"...Behold, the days are coming, says the Lord, when I will make a NEW covenant with the house of Israel and with the house of Judah...For this is the covenant that I will make with the house of Israel: After those days, says the Lord, I will put My laws in their mind and write them on their hearts; and I will be their God, and they shall be My people." Hebrews 8:8,10*

Father, I praise you and thank you for the NEW covenant which you have given to us. I praise you that I cannot claim ignorance of your covenant because you have written and imprinted your laws upon my innermost thoughts and understanding, and you have forever engraved them in my heart. I praise you for the way you have inscribed all of these laws permanently upon my heart, so that wherever I go, I can never get away from you. Hallelujah! I'm a covenant person!

Jan. 23 *"And now I plead with you, lady, not as though I wrote a new commandment to you, but that which we have had from the beginning: that we love one another." II John 5*

Father, how I praise you that you instruct us to live the love-life and walk the love-life. I'm going to walk and talk the love-life at all times and love the unlovely. I praise you for the power you give me to walk this love-walk and for the instructions you give me. Father, let this year be the most loving of my life. I praise you for giving me a special infilling of your precious love.

Jan. 24 *"He who has an ear, let him hear what the Spirit says to the churches. To him who overcomes I will give some of the hidden manna to eat. And I will give him a white stone, and on the stone a new name written which no one knows except him who receives it."* **Rev. 2:17**

Father, I praise you for my ears that hear the Spirit. I thank you for letting me be an overcomer in all things through Christ who strengthens me. I praise you that some day soon I will eat of the hidden manna, and will have a brand new name written in the stone, a name which is just for me. Father, I praise you for your goodness to me. I love you because I don't have to look at the things which are temporal because they are subject to change, but I look at the things which are eternal and lasting. Hallelujah! My ears are hearing, and I'm overcoming.

Jan. 25 *"Then He who sat on the throne said, 'Behold, I make all things new.' And He said to me, 'Write, for these words are true and faithful.' And He said to me, 'It is done! I am the Alpha and the Omega, the Beginning and the End. I will give of the fountain of the water of life freely to him who thirsts. He who overcomes shall inherit all things, and I will be his God and he shall be My son.'"* **Revelation 21:5-7**

Jesus, you are the beginning and the end! Your words are true and faithful! You make all things, including me, brand new! I praise you lavishly because when I was thirsty, you gave to me of the water of life freely. I thank you that because of the power of the Holy Spirit I am an overcomer at all times and because of this I shall inherit all things. God, you are my God, and Jesus, your redemptive work at Calvary made me God's son. Hallelujah!

Jan. 26 *"Knowing this, that our old man was crucified with Him, that the body of sin might be done away with, that we should no longer be slaves of sin. For he who has died has been freed from sin."* **Romans 6:6,7**

Father, how I bless you that with this NEW year,
because of my NEW life, my OLD man is crucified,
lifeless and inanimate, and I don't have to walk under
sin's power and dominion any longer. I praise you
that the old unregenerated, unrenewed man is DEAD,
DEAD, DEAD! Therefore I don't have to serve sin
any longer. Sin is no longer my master. I praise you
that when I learned to die to self, you freed me from
sin, wickedness, impurity, iniquity and error. I am
now a servant to a new master who has revitalized
me in the newness of Christ!

Jan. 27 *"Jesus answered, 'Most assuredly, I say to you, unless one is born of water and the Spirit, he cannot
enter the kingdom of God. That which is born of the
flesh is flesh, and that which is born of the Spirit is
spirit.'" John 3:5,6*

Father, I praise you that I am living in the NEWNESS
of life because I have been born again by your precious
Spirit. I thank you that I am no longer a fleshly creature,
subject to the things of this world, but because I have
been born again, I am a spirit-being under your control.
I praise you that you provided such a beautiful and simple
way for me to have eternal life! I'm walking toward the
kingdom of God with a new lilt in my walk, because
I'm a new creation!

Jan. 28 *"And do not be conformed to this world, but be trans-
formed by the renewing of your mind, that you may
prove what is that good and acceptable and perfect
will of God." Romans 12:2*

Father, I bless you that in my NEW life I do not have
to be conformed to this world. I don't have to dress
the way they do, I don't have to act the way the world
acts, and I don't have to talk the way the world does.
I praise you that my new life gives me freedom to
live the way you want me to. I thank you that my
mind is renewed, with new ideas and ideals and new
attitudes. I bless you for this. I thank you, Father,

that I have presented my body and all its members to you as a living sacrifice, because it is my reasonable and intelligent service to you. I praise you and thank you for your grace which made this all possible. Father, I shall glory in you forever! How perfect are your ways! They are faultless, spotless and unblemished!

Jan. 29 *"Being confident of this very thing, that He who has begun a good work in you will complete it until the day of Jesus Christ." Philippians 1:6*

Father, I praise you for confidence in my NEW life. I bless you that even though I can't always see the end and perfection of what you have planned for me, I have the complete knowledge and faith that you will keep working in me until the day of Jesus Christ. I praise you, Father, that I don't have to worry because you have promised it in your Word! I praise you because you're still working in me and because of this I'm an overcomer, confident that whatever is born of you overcomes the whole world. So I'm going to shout it from the housetops, I'M AN OVER-COMER, I'M AN OVERCOMER because God is working in me!

Jan. 30 *"He has done this through the death on the cross of his own human body, and now as a result Christ has brought you into the very presence of God, and you are standing there before him with nothing left against you--nothing left that he could even chide you for; the only condition is that you fully believe the Truth, standing in it steadfast and firm, strong in the Lord, convinced of the Good News that Jesus died for you, and never shifting from trusting him to save you. This is the wonderful news that came to each of you and is now spreading all over the world. And I, Paul, have the joy of telling it to others." Col. 1:22,23 TLB*

Father, how I praise you that this NEW creature stands before you with nothing left for you to chide me for, because you have buried my sins in the deepest sea never to be remembered again! How I praise you for this. You said the only condition was that I fully believe the Truth and stand in it firmly. Father, I DO, I DO, I DO! I'm standing tall and straight and can look the world straight in the eye, because my sins are gone, gone, GONE!

Jan. 31 *"And we know that all things work together for good to those who love God, to those who are the called according to His purpose." Romans 8:28*

Glory, Father, for the fact that everything, everything, EVERYTHING that happens to me works together for my own good. I thank you that you can take the biggest mess and turn everything in it around so that it turns out for my good. I bless you, Father, that regardless of how dark and gloomy things look, I know beyond a shadow of doubt that it's working for my good. I praise you that when I call for help, the very tide of the battle turns and my enemies flee, all because of you! Thank you that you take any old mess and make a miracle out of it! Thank you, Father, for a month of total victory because I have stood on your promises. Thank you for the extra prosperity that has come into my house; thank you for the health you have given me; thank you for showing me that miracles and wonders still happen these days. Thank you for the marvelous victory you have given me simply by confessing your promises!

═══════ ᵹEBRUARY ═══════

ᵹAITH

The Christian life is so simple because we only have to do two things!
1. Do what God tells us to do.
2. Stop doing what He tells us not to do!

That's all there is to it, and if you do it, you've got it made!

And how do we do what God wants us to do? The Psalmist tells us, *"Your word I have hidden in my heart, that I might not sin against you... (119:11) because Forever, O Lord, Your word is settled in heaven." (119:89)*

Once you establish in your own mind that every single word that is printed on the pages of the Bible is the actual spoken Word of God, and written down for posterity, your faith can begin that upward climb as you read the Word, confess it, memorize it, and hide it in your heart.

How do you increase your faith? *"Faith comes by hearing, and hearing by the word of God" (Romans 10:17)*. We need to HEAR the Word of God.

How can we hear the Word of God? By reading the Bible.

The Bible is God's personal love letter to you, and if you will just read it seeking God, believe it, confess it, and live it, then every promise in the Word is yours!

Feb. 1 *"Now faith is the substance of things hoped for, the evidence of things not seen." Hebrews 11:1*

Thank you, Father, that faith is the pledge and the confirmation of the things we long and hope for, but which we can't see at the moment. We bless you because even though we do not see some things with our natural eyes, in our spirit we can see them as a reality, and because of this, we can see what is not revealed to our senses. Father, I thank you for Noah, who had never heard of rain, and because he was prompted by faith, he diligently constructed and prepared an ark through the eyes of faith. I thank you that in the 20th century I can also look with my eyes of faith and see things come to pass which were just a hope in the past! Hallelujah!

Feb. 2   *"But without faith it is impossible to please Him, for he who comes to God must believe that He is, and that He is a rewarder of those who diligently seek Him." Hebrews 11:6*

Father, thank you for making it so plain that if I don't use the faith you've given me, there is no way I can please you. I bless you, Father, that I don't have to work up something on my own, because your faith is a gift. I believe in you, and I believe that you are the God of all gods! I thank you that you expect me to believe that you are a rewarder of them that diligently seek you. I am and will continue to diligently seek you, and I thank you for rewarding my faith. I bless you that you've made your promises so easy for me to accept through faith! I'm receiving those rewards right now!

Feb. 3   *"Above all, taking the shield of faith, with which you will be able to quench all the fiery darts of the wicked one." Ephesians 6:16*

Thank you, Father, for surrounding me with your shield of faith so that I am completely protected from every kind of wickedness. Any kind of wicked temptation, remark, insult, accusation or attack is quenched and conquered by the shield of faith that I wear constantly, and not even the devil himself can get through it! I walk in the world and I am not afraid. Nothing can harm me. I walk in faith! I talk in faith! I pray in faith and I rejoice in faith! Father, you are my strength and my fortress, and I praise you because with my shield of faith I live in victory **every** minute of the day, every day of the year!

Feb. 4 *"For I say, through the grace given to me, to everyone who is among you, not to think of himself more highly than he ought to think, but to think soberly, as God has dealt to each one a measure of faith." Romans 12:3*

Father, I thank you that you have given to me THE measure of faith I need to be exactly the kind of person you want me to be, and to do ALL the things you want me to do! I praise you because we are all different and distinct individuals and yet you have given to each of us THE same measure of faith as everyone else, so that I can take on the unique tasks that fit in your perfect plan for me. I thank you that you have given me just as much faith as anyone else in the world because all your children are precious to you. I'm using and developing my measure of faith daily, right up to the hilt!

Feb. 5 *"That the sharing of your faith may become effective by the acknowledgment of every good thing which is in you in Christ Jesus." Philemon 6*

My faith produces good fruit in me! Glory! It produces and promotes full recognition, appreciation, understanding and precise knowledge of the fact that when we identify ourselves with the ever-truthful God who cannot deceive, our faith grows and multiplies and abounds! I praise you for a sound mind; for the salvation of my family; for health, wealth and happiness; for joy, love and peace; for prosperity and abundance. I praise you for every good thing! Glory!

Feb. 6 *"I can do all things through Christ who strengthens me." Philippians 4:13*

Thank you for the faith to know that I am empowered through Jesus Christ to do ALL THINGS! I thank you and praise you that I can handle any situation because Jesus strengthens and equips me to succeed in even the most difficult situations and problems which come before me. Through Christ, every obstacle has become a stepping stone for me, every problem an opportunity. Through Christ, I have the willpower to overcome any and all of my bad habits, I thank you because your Word doesn't say I can only do SOME THINGS through Christ which strengthens me, but it says I CAN DO ALL THINGS! Hallelujah, that's power! I thank you that I can live in divine health! I thank you that I can live in prosperity! I thank you that I can live in total victory!

Feb. 7   *"Now the just shall live by faith; but if anyone draws back, My soul has no pleasure in him." Hebrews 10:38*

Glory to God, I'm living by faith! I praise you that your righteous servants shall live by the confident convictions we have regarding man's relationship to you and divine things. I thank you, Father, that we can believe in you, cleave to you and trust in you and because of this we can rely wholly and continually on you through Jesus Christ! I bless you for the warning that if we draw back, you will have no pleasure in us. Father, I'm living in faith, walking in faith, talking in faith and running in faith because I want to please you!

Feb. 8   *"For by grace you have been saved through faith, and that not of yourselves; it is the gift of God." Ephesians 2:8*

I didn't have to save myself! Hallelujah! I thank you, Father, that I didn't do a thing to deserve your unmerited favor, but because of your free grace I have been delivered from judgment and made a partaker of Christ's salvation. I thank you that it was a beautiful gift that you just gave to me, not something that I accomplished by my works or striving; but salvation is mine because you loved me so much that you sent your Son to save me from perishing in the darkness of sin and death. I thank you for that everlasting life I have in Christ. Because you have shown me the fullness of your love, I LOVE YOU, FATHER! I LOVE YOUR SON, JESUS CHRIST! I LOVE THE NEW LIFE YOU HAVE GIVEN ME THROUGH YOUR BELOVED SON!

Feb. 9 *"Giving thanks to the Father who has qualified us to be partakers of the inheritance of the saints in the light. He has delivered us from the power of darkness and translated us into the kingdom of the Son of His love." Colossians 1:12,13*

I will thank you and praise you forever, Father, because I AM DELIVERED! I've been taken out of the control and the dominion of darkness, changed so that I am qualified to share the inheritance of the saints, and translated into the kingdom of light! Glorious Father, how I praise you that because of your loving kindness and mercy I have been made a partaker of the inheritance of all the saints! Glory, I've been delivered from bad habits, evil thoughts, and delivered from the very power of the devil! I want to say THANK YOU, THANK YOU, THANK YOU because you have reached inside of me and turned me into a brand new person, and you have sent me straight into the kingdom of your beloved Son, Jesus Christ!

Feb. 10 *"Rejoice in the Lord always. Again I will say, rejoice!" Philippians 4:4*

How can I thank you enough for all the wonderful reasons I have to rejoice in you, Father? I rejoice in your Presence in my life! I rejoice in each new day you give me to live, to love, to enjoy and to help others! I rejoice that I am your child and that you love me more than I love myself! I rejoice in your Word, in your power, in your glory! I rejoice in the blessings you shower upon me day after day — blessings of joy, of health, of prosperity, of family and of friends! I rejoice in the work you give me to do and in the quiet times in my day when I come to you and worship you. I rejoice when I'm tired, I rejoice in you even when I am attacked by the devil. I delight in you even when my body is not up to par. I rejoice at night. I rejoice during the day! God, you are really fabulous!

Feb. 11   *"Even the righteousness of God which is through faith in Jesus Christ to all and on all who believe. For there is no difference;" Romans 3:22*

Glory to God! I have the RIGHTEOUSNESS OF GOD in me because I have faith and personal trust in Jesus Christ! I praise you, Father, that your righteousness is available to everyone who believes in and confidently relies on Jesus, because that means I'm conformed to your Word and your promise! I'm rejoicing RIGHT NOW that I am marching in accordance with your plan! Thank you for filling me with your righteousness, because I'm using that loving righteousness with my family, my friends and the people I work with every day. Father, I love your righteousness!

Feb. 12   *"For I am persuaded that neither death nor life, nor angels nor principalities nor powers, nor things present nor things to come, nor height nor depth, nor any other created thing, shall be able to separate us from the love of God which is in Christ Jesus our Lord." Romans 8:38,39*

Father, my faith is rising to new heights! I thank you that I am in your love and that nothing, ABSOLUTELY NOTHING, CAN EVER SEPARATE ME FROM YOUR LOVE! I'm overwhelmed that your Word has made it so clear, so powerfully plain and positive that I can never be moved from your love which is in Christ Jesus our Lord. Right this very second I rejoice that your power guarantees me your eternal love, no matter what the devil or any of his demons try to pull, any time or any place. I'm living in your divine love, regardless of any and all circumstances!

Feb. 13 *"I have been crucified with Christ; it is no longer I who live, but Christ lives in me; and the life which I now live in the flesh I live by faith in the Son of God, who loved me and gave Himself for me." Gal. 2:20*

Glory to God. I'm dead and alive at the same time! Thank you, precious Father, that I'm living a life that is really Jesus Christ living in me! I praise you, Father, because my worldly ways and sins were crucified on the cross with Jesus, who loved me and gave himself for me. The old me is dead – doubts, thoughts, habits, hurts and memories – and I'm a completely new person, top to bottom, inside and out. The body life I live is now ruled by Jesus, and I live in this body of flesh and bone by my faith in him. Because of this, I'm a new person with nothing to hold me back! Father, I thank you that my new life glorifies you!

Feb. 14 *"For God so loved the world that He gave His only begotten Son, that whoever believes in Him should not perish but have everlasting life." John 3:16*

Father, this is the day the world says is the day for lovers, but I don't have to depend on just one day a year, because I'm living in your love every single day of the year. Thank you that your love encompasses the entire world, and yet is personal just for me. I praise you because my Bible has my name in it, and not just the words "the world." It actually has my name in it. Father, you said if I would simply believe in you, I would not perish, but have everlasting life. I BELIEVE, I BELIEVE, I BELIEVE! Thank you for the faith that lets me believe!

Feb. 15 *"If anyone speaks, let him speak as the oracles of God. If anyone ministers, let him do it as with the ability which God supplies, that in all things God* *may be glorified through Jesus Christ, to whom belong the glory and the dominion forever and ever. Amen." I Peter 4:11*

Father, I bless you that as I speak, I speak as a prophet of God, because my mouth shall speak your words. I thank you that pleasant words are as an honeycomb, sweet to the soul and health to the bones. I praise you because I have a wholesome tongue which is a tree of life: I bless you that my mouth is also as a well of life. I guard my tongue so that I am not snared with the words of my mouth. My heart retains your words, and out of the abundance of my heart, filled with your words, shall I speak! Glory!

Feb. 16 *"Casting all your care upon Him, for He cares for you." I Peter 5:7*

Here are my cares, Father! This means ALL of my worries, anxieties and concern. I'm giving them all to you, once and for all! Your love overwhelms me! I praise and thank you for taking all of my worries and cares away because you love me so much you don't want me to be burdened. My anxieties are gone! I bless you because your Word works! Just as in the story of the prodigal son, you don't care what I've done or what I've been, you love me and care for me. Father, I'm so glad to be home at last with you. I rejoice because I'm your child, forgiven, restored by your mercy and loving kindness to my inheritance in your kingdom. I praise you, Father, that my ways have been changed because you care for me! Glory! I don't have any more worries!

Feb. 17 *"I will give you a new heart and put a new spirit within you; I will take the heart of stone out of your flesh and give you a heart of flesh." Ezekiel 36:26*

Father, I'm so thankful that I have a new heart and a new spirit within me! Thank you, Father, that you've taken my stony heart out and replaced it with a heart filled to the brim with love! I love you! I love my friends! I love my family! I even love my enemies because of what you have done for me! I never have to worry about running out of love because you keep filling me up with more, more, more! I thank you, Father, that I can love you with all of this new heart you've given me, and I thank you that with my new spirit I now live righteously.

Feb. 18 *"Then Jesus spoke to them again, saying, 'I am the light of the world. He who follows Me shall not walk in darkness, but have the light of life.'" John 8:12*

It's fun walking in the light, Father, because Jesus is the light of the world! Thank you, Father, for the light you gave me through your Son, Jesus, because by his wonderful, brilliant light I walked out of the gloom of darkness and left it behind forever! Now I can see the way, because the path of new life in Jesus shines with His wonderful light! I praise and glorify you, Father, for sending us the light of the world! Darkness holds no more fear for me because it's gone from my life and I am walking and leaping and praising God in the Light! I glory in the light of Jesus and I follow where He leads me. In His light I am happy, I am healthy, I am prosperous! In His light I am fulfilled and victorious! His light IS my life!

Feb. 19 *"If any of you lacks wisdom, let him ask of God, who gives to all liberally and without reproach, and it will be given to him." James 1:5*

I praise you, Father, because I have wisdom! I have all the wisdom I need to prevail over any challenge, because your Word says if I don't have it, all I have to do is ask and it will be given to me by you, liberally and ungrudgingly. I thank you for giving me the kind of wisdom that triumphs over worldly knowledge every time, because worldly knowledge can't hold a candle to your wisdom. I thank you because you are a giving God, so I have all the wisdom I need to live and work and make decisions righteously and victoriously. I have wisdom in all my dealings with my fellow man and I praise and thank you for it!

Feb. 20 *"Let your conduct be without covetousness, and be content with such things as you have. For He Himself has said, I will never leave you nor forsake you. So we may boldly say: The Lord is my helper; I will not fear. What can man do to me?" Hebrews 13:5,6*

I am gloriously satisfied, Father, in the overflowing abundance of divine blessings you have showered upon my life! I am content in your love! I praise you that there just isn't any room left in me for greed or for envy of what my neighbors have, because your constant presence in my life is wealth far above the material things of this world. I'm not afraid of what anybody can do to me because you've assured me that you are my helper, and who could possibly prevail over my all-powerful God? Father, I don't have to rely on worldly security, because YOU ARE EVERYTHING I NEED! I praise you because you never relax your hold on me. You never let me go! Glory!

Feb. 21 *"For assuredly, I say to you, whoever says to this mountain, 'Be removed and be cast into the sea,' and does not doubt in his heart, but believes that those things he says will come to pass, he will have whatever he says." Mark 11:23*

Jesus, I believe, I believe, I believe! Because I obey you, I believe from the bottom of my heart that your Word and your promise empower me to have anything I desire when I pray. What I say shall take place. Therefore, I say I have wisdom! I have health! I have happiness! I have prosperity! I have an abundance! I have joy! I have love! Father, I say to that mountain in my life, "get lost and fall into the sea," because I believe your promise that I can have whatsoever I say. (Move your mountain right now!)

Feb. 22 *"Therefore I say to you, whatever things you ask when you pray, believe that you receive them, and you will have them."* **Mark 11:24**

Father, I believe RIGHT NOW! I've prayed, and the minute the words came out of my mouth. I BELIEVED! I thank you, Father, that you didn't tell me to wait until I built up enough faith to believe, but to believe the very instant I prayed, so that I could have the things that I desired. I praise you, Father, that because I take delight in you, you give me the desires of my heart, and that's why I know that I know that I KNOW that you're going to fulfill the desires that you yourself have placed there! Glory, Father, thank you for the faith you've given to me!

Feb. 23 *"...If anyone is thirsty, let him come to me and drink. For the Scriptures declare that rivers of living water shall flow from the inmost being of anyone who believes in me."* **John 7:37,38 TLB**

Father, I'm thirsty, thirsty, thirsty! I'm drinking at your streams of living water deeper and deeper all the time. I bless you because that same river of living water that I'm drinking now blesses me and blesses everyone around me as it flows from my innermost being. Father, I praise you for giving to us a river of living water that never runs dry, but keeps flowing and flowing. Thank you for that refilling station you've given me to use day and night. Thank you because it is open 24 hours a day. Father, I love you for that!

Feb. 24 *"You can be very sure that the evil man will not go unpunished forever. And you can also be very sure God will rescue the children of the godly."* **Proverbs 11:21 TLB**

Father, how I praise you for such a promise. My faith is in you, and not in what I see, because as I look at my children, sometimes I feel like giving up, but you've promised that you will rescue my children, and how I love you for that. Thank you that my family is on your favored list, because you have promised that my household will be saved! I'm rejoicing in that. I thank you, Father, because *the wicked are overthrown, and are no more, but the house of the righteous will stand,* (Proverbs 12:7) so my house is standing on the promises of your Word. I praise you that I am godly only because I have been born again of incorruptible seed. Hallelujah!

Feb. 25 *"For this reason we also, since the day we heard it, do not cease to pray for you, and to ask that you may be filled with the knowledge of His will in all wisdom and spiritual understanding; that you may have a walk worthy of the Lord, fully pleasing Him, being fruitful in every good work and increasing in the knowledge of God." Colossians 1:9,10*

Father, I praise you that I am being filled with the knowledge of your will in all wisdom and spiritual understanding. I thank you that I am constantly learning your ways and purposes and that you are giving me discernment of spiritual things. I praise you that because you have given me these blessings, I am walking worthy of you Lord, being fruitful in every good work and steadily growing and increasing in my knowledge of you. I thank you that all my decisions are ordered by you! Glory!

Feb. 26 *"And now I am coming to you. I have told them many things while I was with them so that they would be filled with my joy." John 17:13 TLB*

Father, I bless you because I am filled with joy! The joy of the Lord is my strength, so I'm strong because my cup is filled to the top and overflowing with joy. I bless you because you have anointed me with the oil of gladness. I sing and shout with joy because I have favor with God and man, so I'm always a winner. I bless you because my joy is contagious and flows over to reach others, and today I'm speaking love, joy and peace to everyone I meet. Thank you for telling me the things which have put joy in my heart! Glory, I'm bubbling, bubbling, bubbling over!

Feb. 27 *"Having been born again, not of corruptible seed but incorruptible, through the word of God which lives and abides forever." I Peter 1:23*

I'm born again of incorruptible seed! Father, I can't thank and praise you enough for lifting me out of the darkness and sin of the world, where mortal life leads only to death. By your Word, I am made new, regenerated, reborn to eternal life in your kingdom. I am in this world of corruption and decay, but I am not of it because the perfect seed of your Word has made me into an entirely new person. Father, I praise you that your Word lives and abides forever! Because of this, I shall live forever, too! Glory!

Feb. 28 *"The Spirit Himself bears witness with our spirit that we are children of God, and if children, then heirs – heirs of God and joint heirs with Christ, if indeed we suffer with Him, that we may also be glorified together." Romans 8:16,17*

Father, how I thank you for letting me know in no uncertain terms that I can never be lost or alone because the Holy Spirit says that I AM your child! I know where I belong. Bless you, Father, that I am a joint-heir with Jesus, and you gave everything you had to Him, so I share fully in the entire inheritance. Father, I'm so rich because of your promises. I praise you that because I am a joint-heir with Jesus, I am your temple, because your Spirit dwells in me! I thank you that I have power to overcome all obstacles in this world. You are my God, I am your child, and I claim your promise that all things in heaven and earth belong to me!

Feb. 29 *"Therefore I say to you, do not worry about your life, what you will eat or what you will drink; nor about*

your body, what you will put on. Is not life more than
food and the body more than clothing?" Matthew 6:25

Thank you, Father, for another beautiful month. A
month where I had the opportunity to love you more
than ever before; a month where I had the opportunity to study and grow in your Word. Father, your
Word, your promises, have become real in my life in
ways that make me love you more and more. I thank
you that your Word endures forever and that I have
victory. I don't have to take thought for my life because my life is in you, Father, and you supply EV-
ERYTHING! I thank you that the kingdom of God is
not meat and drink, but righteousness and peace and
joy in the Holy Ghost. I have health! I have prosperity! I have joy! I have peace! I have Jesus!

ℙROSPERITY

Mar. 1 *"Beloved, I pray that you may prosper in all things and be in health, just as your soul prospers." III John 2*

My soul is prospering! Father, I rejoice that the wish you have for me, high above all others, is prosperity and health for both my body and my soul! Glory, how I thank you for being such a wonderful and loving Father, who takes care of me in such full and overflowing measure. Thank you for the secret of prosperity which lies in giving to you so that you can multiply it back to me. I'm not going to hold tight to what I have, Father, but instead I'm keeping my hands empty and open so you can keep filling them up with more! And, I'm placing the same trust in you for my health, Father, knowing how generously you provide. Thank you for the blessing of wonderful and divine health that I live in all this year. Your Word is my life, so my soul is prospering!

Mar. 2 *"Bring the whole tithe into the storehouse, that there may be food in my house. Test me in this," says the Lord Almighty, "and see if I will not throw open the floodgates of heaven and pour out so much blessing that you will not have room enough for it." Malachi 3:10 NIV*

Here it is, Father, my whole tithe. I'm giving it to you! I praise you, Father, for being the best financial advisor I could possibly have! I'm giving generously into your storehouse, Almighty Father, because it pleases you to "throw open the floodgates of heaven" and to let the blessings gush out in abundance upon us. I am made in your image, so I know you want me to be generous even as you are generous in giving to me until I have no room for more! I receive the gift of your blessed abundance with thanks and praise, and I'm giving to you, Father, fully trusting in your promise of return. I'm expanding my mind and my ability to receive your blessings to make more room for that flood that is pouring out of those floodgates.

Mar. 3   *"To the man who pleases him, God gives wisdom, knowledge and happiness, but to the sinner he gives the task of gathering and storing up wealth to hand it over to the one who pleases God." Ecc. 2:26 NIV*

The sinner is my slave! Even if he owns a den of iniquity, he is working to gather and store up money to give to the righteous who are in right standing with you. Glory! I thank you that you have given me wisdom, knowledge and happiness to know this! I rejoice because you teach us that covetousness and greed are meaningless, for you take the wealth sinners have gained and give it to those who please you, for your way is righteousness. I receive that sinner's money right now! I'm blessed by your marvelous generosity, Father. Keep that sinner working so I can have more to give to you!

Mar. 4   *"Cast your bread upon the waters, for you will find it after many days." Ecclesiastes 11:1*

Heavenly Father, I love to cast my bread upon your waters and I praise you for the way you multiply it and send back many times over what I give! Thanks for showing me that the real secret of receiving is to give with a loving heart, because when I put my whole trust in you, everything always comes back magnified! Father, I thank you that I am able to give love, kindness, a helping hand, time, money, and gifts whenever you tell me to because it's your good pleasure to replace it to me from your own unlimited storehouse. I've cast my bread upon the water, Father, and I thank you for the cinnamon buns that are coming back. Thank you for the danish. Thank you for the doughnuts. Thank you that the whole bakery is coming back to me!

Mar. 5 *"But seek first the kingdom of God and His righteousness, and all these things shall be added to you." Matthew 6:33*

ALL THINGS? Father, I praise and thank you for the truth of the promises in your Word! You said ALL THINGS shall be added to me, and I believe every word of it! I am craving and earnestly seeking everything in the kingdom of God. You never fail me, for you have gathered me into your kingdom and your righteousness, and here I am, jubilantly rejoicing because of it! You give me everything I need, not because of what I do or don't do, but because I'm a member of your very own family, loved and cared for, from now through eternity. I hold out my hands to you, Father, and claim your promise that ALL things are added to me. I have love, joy, peace of mind, health and prosperity. I have ALL things! Father, you're so good to me that I can't glorify you enough!

Mar. 6 *"For the Lord God is a sun and shield; the Lord will give grace and glory; no good thing will He withhold from those who walk uprightly." Psalm 84:11*

I don't need sunglasses, Father, because you are my shield! I love you for promising that you will not withhold one single good thing from me. I rejoice to walk uprightly in your light because in your light I can always know how to handle any situation. Your shield protects me from the devil's barbs, his lies, his deceits, and I rejoice that he runs at breakneck speed away from your light! Protected by your shield, illumined by your light, my life is blessed by an abundance of your gifts, for you are a God of grace and glory! I glorify your name, Father, because you supply all my needs and more! Thank you for the heavenly bliss and favor you generously bestow on me. I confidently commit all I am and all I have to you!

Mar. 7   *"Give, and it will be given to you: good measure, pressed down, shaken together, and running over will be put into your bosom. For with the same measure that you use, it will be measured back to you." Luke 6:38*

Father, how I bless you for your money-back guarantee which guarantees that when I give to you, it shall be given back to me. When I give love, you give me an exceeding abundance of love. When I give time, you return that time to me over and over again. When I give money, you give it back to me in full and overflowing and plenteous amounts. I praise you that you use what I give as a measuring spoon to dish out what you give to me, so I don't ever need to be limited by anything except what I am willing to give. Father, I'm giving my all and everything I am and all my possessions to you, and I thank you that I am walking in a super abundant supply!

Mar. 8   *"But remember this – if you give little, you will get little. A farmer who plants just a few seeds will get only a small crop, but if he plants much, he will reap much." II Corinthians 9:6 TLB*

How I praise you, Father, for the wonderful harvest you are bringing forth in my garden! Thank you for teaching me how to be a successful farmer. Thank you for teaching me to sow generously and joyfully in great abundance so you can bless it and return it to me multiplied beyond my wildest dreams! Thank you for the harvest you have prepared for me. Thank you for teaching me not to be stingy in any area of my life, whether it's in love, health, joy, or finances. I plant in faith, generously – and you open the floodgates of heaven to pour blessings on me! I thank and praise you, Father, for the exploding abundance of all things you bring about from the seeds of my giving!

Mar. 9 *"Do not gather and heap up and store for yourselves treasures on earth, where moth and rust and worm consume and destroy, and where thieves break through and steal; But gather and heap up and store for yourselves treasures in heaven, where neither moth nor rust nor worm consume and destroy, and where thieves do not break through and steal; For where your treasure is, there will your heart be also." Matt. 6:19-21 Amp.*

No thanks, I don't need any mothballs today! I'm not storing my treasures up here on the earth, but I'm storing them up in heaven with you, Father, where I don't have to worry about moths and rust or even thieves who break through and steal. Father, I'm banking my treasure with you because you are the most reliable trust company in the entire world. You are a living river of blessings, and I praise you for taking care of your children with loving interest! My treasure is in heaven with you, and my heart is right up there, too!

Mar. 10 *"And my God shall supply all your need according to His riches in glory by Christ Jesus." Philippians 4:19*

My needs are gloriously and liberally supplied! Thank you, Father, for sending Jesus to die on the cross as a ransom for my sins because through Him I have abundant new life! I praise you not only for paying all my bills, but also for taking care of me in countless invisible ways – providing love when I need it, lifting my spirit, sending a friend when I need a helping hand, directing your angels to guard my family. Over and over, you surprise me with your miraculous timing in providing answers to even unspoken prayers of mine! Father, I rejoice that my needs are faithfully and constantly fulfilled from your wonderful and inexhaustible riches in glory by Christ Jesus!

Mar. 11 *"The bin of flour was not used up, nor did the jar of oil run dry, according to the word of the Lord which He spoke by Elijah." I Kings 17:16*

My cruse of oil shall never fail, because I shall never eat my seed! I praise you, Father, that when the widow was willing to listen to your prophet and share what she had instead of eating it all with her son, that you kept filling the barrel of meal and pouring oil into the cruse. Father, how we bless you for giving us instructions on how to have sufficient at all times. I praise you that even though the supply looks low at times, I can rest assured that you're always there to put in what I need!

Mar. 12 *"I love those who love me, and those who seek me diligently will find me. Riches and honor are with me, enduring riches and righteousness. My fruit is better than gold, yes, than fine gold, and my revenue than choice silver. I traverse the way of righteousness, in the midst of the paths of justice, that I may cause those who love me to inherit wealth, that I may fill their treasuries." Proverbs 8:17-21*

Father, how I love your Word and all the promises you have for me. I thank you that enduring wealth and uprightness in every area and relationship, and right standing with you is mine! I thank you that you even allow me to inherit substance, often from sources I never knew about, and that you fill my treasures and that I am indeed wealthy, because my riches are heavenly and divine. Thank you that you have taken charge of my earthly bank account and filled it with divine deposits! Glory!

Mar. 13 *"The curse of the Lord is on the house of the wicked, but He blesses the habitation of the just." Prov. 3:33*

Father, my house is blessed! I rejoice that you are a God of justice, that no thought or act escapes your notice, that you know which are the houses of the wicked and which are the houses of the righteous. You see through all the deceptions of the wicked; there is no way they can hide from your curse. But I praise you, that you also see directly into the hearts and minds of the righteous and you never forget to bless and reward your children who serve you faithfully. Look into my heart and my mind, dear Father, because I rejoice in praising you! I glory in your wonderful blessings!

Mar. 14 *"The blessing of the Lord makes one rich, and He adds no sorrow with it." Proverbs 10:22*

I praise you, Father, for filling my life with the treasure of your blessing, which makes me rejoice day after day. I am rich in you! I am rich in your endless love, which feeds me like manna from heaven! You put the food on my table, the clothes on my back, the smiles on my children's faces! Glory, Father, how can I thank you enough? You give me health, happiness and prosperity! You guard me from temptation and teach me with the wisdom of your Word! You renew and refresh my spirit so I can face each day with joy! Father, I praise you for not adding sorrow to my life, because with all your blessings, there just isn't room for it!

Mar. 15 *"And I say to you, ask, and it will be given to you; seek, and you will find; knock, and it will be opened to you. For everyone who asks receives, and he who seeks finds, and to him who knocks it will be opened." Luke 11;9,10*

Glory, hallelujah, Father, I'm an asker, a seeker and a knocker, and because of this, I'm a receiver. Thank you that your Word says if I ask it shall be given to me! Thank you that you didn't say SOME will receive but you said EVERY ONE, and that includes me! Father, I praise you because when I ask, YOU give to me; when I knock, YOU open the door; when I seek, YOU guide me safely to my destination. I'm asking, Father, and therefore I have what I ask for. I have love! I have joy! I have health! I have prosperity! Thank you for being such a loving and generous Father to me!

Mar. 16 *"He has given food to those who fear Him; He will ever be mindful of His covenant." Psalm 111:5*

Oh, glorious Father, you are the river of life, the provider of all my well-being! I rejoice every day because you remember me without fail. You not only put the meat on my table but you nourish my soul and protect me from all physical harm, because I am your child, and you love me. I eat the meat you give me with a hearty appetite, delighting in each bite because I know who has provided it and who will always provide it. Father, I am thankful for everything you give me, for it all belongs to you, and I am blessed by your caring, sharing, loving, wonderful faithfulness to me! Hallelujah! I praise you that your covenant is forever imprinted on your mind so that you will remember it throughout all of eternity.

Mar. 17 *"The Lord is my shepherd; I shall not want." Ps. 23:1*

I shall not want for health! I shall not want for finances! Father, do you know what gets me so excited about your promises? They are magnificent, BIG promises! You just don't give out small, stingy promises to your children, because your LOVE FOR US IS SO GREAT THAT YOU WANT US TO HAVE THE WHOLE WORKS! I thank you and praise you, heavenly Father, because you say plainly and clearly that I shall not want! You are my God, and I am your child! You are my shepherd, and I follow where you lead! I rejoice because you are the kind of Father who wants me to personally prosper in this life and to share your eternal glory in the next! Father, I'm blessed beyond words! I shall not want for joy! I shall not want for happiness! Glory!

Mar. 18 *"Blessed be the Lord, who daily loads us with benefits, the God of our salvation! Selah" Psalm 68:19*

I'm loaded, but not with problems, Father! I thank you for loading me with the good things of life every day! I don't have to live on yesterday's blessings or wait for tomorrow's blessings, because you send fresh new blessings each day. I'm singing and shouting my praises up to you because you give me a taste of heaven right on this earth! You are the God of my salvation, and all glory belongs to you. Every moment of this day is special to me because you are always right here with me, and you know what benefits I need much better than I do! I love you, praise you and bless your name, Father, for all I'm receiving today. It's all so good, you can just keep loading me down! Thank you that I don't have to have monthly or weekly blessings, but that you supply them on a daily basis! Hallelujah!

Mar. 19 *"Yes, the Lord will give what is good; and our land will yield its increase." Psalm 85:12*

I can't help praising you, Father, because you know how to give good gifts. You have given me life and you have removed the curse of sin from my life through the sacrifice of your only begotten Son on the cross. I thank you for my new life and my salvation. I thank you for Jesus Christ. I thank you for the Holy Spirit. Yes, Father, you give what is good, and my heart rejoices, my arms open wide, to receive your gifts! I love you with all my heart, all my soul, all my mind and all my strength. Because of your goodness, Father, our land is blessed with a rich harvest, and I am prospered.

Mar. 20 *"And all these blessings shall come upon you and overtake you, if you heed the voice of the Lord your God." Deuteronomy 28:2 Amp.*

I'm ready, Father, to be overcome and overtaken with blessings! I've listened to the devil too long, but from now on I'm listening to your voice only. I've cleaned out my ears and I'm hearing even the tiniest little word you say to me. I'm singing your praises and rejoicing because you've promised that your blessings will catch up with me and simply overwhelm me. I can hardly wait! I want to peek over my shoulder and watch them arrive, Father, because I've inherited even the blessings you gave to Abraham, because Jesus took my sins away so that I might be restored to your favor. I praise you for the abiding love you have for your people which has flowed down through the centuries to reach me. I bless you because I live under your blessings. I heard the condition to your blessings, too, Father, so I'm doing my part and following your instructions completely!

Mar. 21 *"Blessed shall you be in the city, and blessed shall you be in the field." Deuteronomy 28:3 Amp.*

Heavenly Father, you know what our cities are like and You know what it's like to be a farmer these days, so I rejoice that your blessing follows me wherever I go! I thank you that you are my shield and protection from evil in the city! I thank you that you are my strength and my rest in the field! You are with me wherever I go, so that my way is blessed and prosperous, my work goes well, and my life bears fruit that pleases you. Because you love and bless me I am not swallowed up in the confusion and darkness of the world. I rejoice, Father, because you are with me!

Mar. 22 *"Blessed shall be your basket and your kneading trough." Deuteronomy 28:5 Amp.*

How I rejoice, Father, that I don't have to worry about inflation, the price of food and shopping. I praise you that complex economic policies, the rise and fall of the stock market and business red tape don't have any effect on your blessings. Heavenly Father, when you say my basket is blessed, IT IS BLESSED! My kneading trough, or my bread, is blessed because I'm feasting on Jesus, the bread of life! Your blessings come as promises, IN POWER AND IN TRUTH!

You are my God, and nations rise and decay under your hand, but your blessings remain with me through thick and thin! Father, I've forgotten how to worry because I'm too busy praising and thanking you to have time for it!

Mar. 23 *"Blessed shall you be when you come in, and blessed shall you be when you go out." Deut. 28:6 Amp.*

I'm blessed coming in, and I'm blessed going out! Glory, Father, when I knock on the door, you open it so I can come in and I am blessed! When I go out to seek, you help me to find what I'm seeking, and again I'm blessed! Father, only through you am I assured of getting blessed whether I'm coming or going! I praise you, heavenly Father, FOR DIRECTING MY WAY, because in your glorious wisdom, I am guided to the door of opportunities that bless me, and I am guided out the door to better opportunities that bless me again. I rejoice and thank you, Father, that you care for me enough to always bless my coming in and going out.

Mar. 24 *"The Lord shall cause your enemies who rise up against you to be defeated before your face; they shall come out against you one way, and flee before you seven ways." Deuteronomy 28:7 Amp.*

Enemies, get ready to go! I thank you, Father, that those who come against me with evil in their hearts will never find me alone, but always with you. I praise you because in your righteousness and power, you defeat my enemies and strike confusion into their ranks, so that they run before me seven different ways! Father, even when I am under attack, I'm still blessed – because I stand firm and glorify you before the world for causing the defeat of unrighteousness. Thank you, heavenly Father, for blessing me under all conditions! I can't lose with you, Father, because I'm blessed when they attack me, and I'm blessed when they leave me alone!

Mar. 25 *"The Lord shall command the blessing upon you in your storehouse, and in all that you undertake; and He will bless you in the land which the Lord your God gives you." Deuteronomy 28:8 Amp.*

Everything I undertake is blessed – what a promise! Father, I praise you because when you command something to be done, IT IS DONE! Thank you for commanding a blessing upon me, personally, for the projects I've already started, and the things I'm going to do in the future. Father, I work with your praises upon my lips, because you bless and reward those who are faithful to you. I don't worry about my savings, because your blessing protects what is mine better than any bank vault. I'm not anxious about the success of anything I tackle, because under your blessing my work prospers! Father, you have blessed me in everything you have given me, and I am grateful to you! Hallelujah!

Mar. 26 *"And the Lord shall make you have a surplus of prosperity, through the fruit of your body, of your livestock, and of your ground, in the land which the Lord swore to your fathers to give you." Deut. 28:11 Amp.*

Thank you, Father, that your Word promises more than bare sufficiency, your Word promises PLENTEOUS GOODS! I rejoice and praise you because your plan for me is a life of abundance, not just scraping by day-to-day. I thank you because everything I do multiplies and bears fruit in the power of your generous and loving blessing upon me and upon my land. Father, you are a fountain of blessings to me, and I glorify your name! I have more than enough and I will always have an excess, an oversupply and a balance left over to give to others in need! Hallelujah!

Mar. 27 *"The Lord shall open to you His good treasury..." Deut. 28:12 Amp.*

Father, when I think that you open to me your good treasury, that means everything you've got is open and available to me. I feel like a child, full of excitement, sticking my hand in a grab bag of goodies! Some things in a grab bag are disappointing, but Father, ALL of the things in your treasury are good! I rejoice because it is truly your pleasure to give me the kingdom. I bless you, Father, because when you open something up, you don't open just a little crack or a little chink, but you open the whole thing up. I thank you and rejoice that you are the one who's doing it, Father, and that you don't make me try to chisel my way inside of something difficult to get inside of, but you just open it up to me, free of charge. How I love you for your generosity!

Mar. 28 *"A good man leaves an inheritance [of moral stability and goodness] to his children's children, and the wealth of the sinner [finds its way eventually] into the hands of the righteous, for whom it was laid up." Proverbs 13:22 Amp.*

Heavenly Father, I thank you that I am leaving an inheritance of moral values and good behavior to my children and my children's children, both through the example I set for them and through teaching them your Word. I glorify you, Father, because you don't allow the sinner's ways to go unpunished, for you take the sinner's money and pass it into the hands of those who love you. You are a God of justice and righteousness, because your Word says, "the wages of sin is death," and you bring the sinner's inheritance to nothing. Father, I lift my hands up right now to be a funnel for you to pour the sinner's wealth into me, and I receive your prosperity.

Mar. 29 *"Roll your works upon the Lord – commit and trust them wholly to Him; [He will cause your thoughts to become agreeable to His will, and] so shall your plans be established and succeed." Proverbs 16:3 Amp.*

My plans are established and succeeding! What a promise! I praise you, Father, because when I bring my intentions and plans and ideas to you before I start on any project, you conform my thoughts to your will so that everything I do succeeds wonderfully. I thank you because even if I come to you with wrong ideas, and roll them all upon you, trusting and committing them to your precious care, you just turn my thoughts around so that I think in the right direction. I'm letting all of my thoughts go right straight to you because without you, my thoughts could go off on all kinds of tangents and get me into trouble, but with you my plans are established and succeeding! Hallelujah!

Mar. 30 *"No weapon formed against you shall prosper, and every tongue which rises against you in judgment you shall condemn. This is the heritage of the servants of the Lord, and their righteousness is from Me, says the Lord." Isaiah 54:17*

Father, I rejoice that my heritage in you protects me from the weapons of enemies and the tongues of the wicked or mistaken people who speak against me. My righteousness is in you, so I have nothing to fear. The devil and his deceptions are turned away from me and are brought to nothing by your power because my faith is in you, and you are my shield and my buckler. Thank you for wrapping your shield of faith around me so that I can confidently face the world and know that no weapon of any kind that is formed against me can prosper in any way because of your Word! Glory!

Mar. 31 *"So shall My word be that goes forth from My mouth; it shall not return to Me void* (empty, without fruit), *but it shall accomplish what I please, and it shall prosper in the thing for which I sent it." Isaiah 55:11*

Glory, Father, that your Word goes forth with POWER, AND DOES WHAT YOU INTEND IT TO DO! I thank you because your promises and your blessings prosper me and my works, exactly as you want them to. I thank you for your loving kindness, for the many blessings you have poured out upon me this month and for your constant presence in my life. I praise you because you are a God of power and glory and righteousness and because the Word that goes forth from your mouth with such wonderful authority brings me joy, peace, love, happiness, friendship, health and prosperity as I let those same words flow through my mouth!

ꝮHE ꝯAME OF ꝯESUS!

Confess this every day this month, along with the one for each particular day, to firmly establish in your mind that HE IS RISEN:

"Thank you, Father, that we can say HE IS RISEN because when they went to the tomb, He was not there! It was EMPTY! Thank you that in spite of the fact that He died on the cross and took ALL of the sins and filth of mankind upon Himself, He established forever that the NAME OF JESUS was above all other names when He arose victoriously out of the bonds of hell and over the power of Satan. Thank you, Father, for the resurrection power that made salvation possible."

Each day as you make your confession, whether you are alone or with someone, say it out loud, and say it with authority until the confession that is written becomes YOUR confession!

Apr. 1   *"Therefore God also has highly exalted Him and given Him the name which is above every name, that at the name of Jesus every knee should bow, of those in heaven, and of those on earth, and of those under the earth, and that every tongue should confess that Jesus Christ is Lord, to the glory of God the Father." Philippians 2:9-11*

Jesus, Jesus, Jesus. How I love that name! I bless you, Father, for giving your Son such a beautiful name. Thank you for your power in that name. I praise you that the name of Jesus is over and above sickness, disease, poverty, demons, and everything else the devil tries to give me. I take the name of Jesus over any plague that tries to come near my dwelling,

because that name is above all things inside and out.
My tongue confesses daily that Jesus Christ is Lord.
Jesus is Lord! JESUS IS LORD!

Apr.2 *"Then He arose and rebuked the wind, and said to
the sea, 'Peace, be still!' And the wind ceased and
there was a great calm." Mark 4:39*

Father, how we bless you that at the name of Jesus,
the wildest storm that may be blowing around us has
to be still and quiet. I praise you that when that old
enemy comes in like a flood, the name of Jesus
muzzles whatever the devil is trying to do. My heart
shall have peace all day today because whenever the
wind starts to blow again, I shall take the name of
Jesus on my lips. Thank you for the peace that passes
all understanding that rests in my heart because of
what you've given to us in the NAME of Jesus!

Apr. 3 *"That the name of our Lord Jesus Christ may be glorified in you, and you in Him, according to the grace of
our God and the Lord Jesus Christ." II Thess. 1:12*

Father, it has been nearly 2,000 years since you sent
your Son to walk on this earth. I'm bubbling over
and still can't stop talking about His wonderful miraculous life and I still can't thank you and praise
you enough for sending Him. I thank and praise you
for giving me the opportunity to have Jesus glorified
in me by the way I live my life before all the world,
and to be glorified even myself because I live in Him.
Thank you, Father, because this can only happen by
your grace and that of our Lord Jesus Christ. Thank
you for that beautiful name above all names, the name
of Jesus! I take it upon my lips daily in thanksgiving
for what you have done for me.

Apr. 4 *"And the whole multitude sought to touch Him, for power
went out from Him and healed them all." Luke 6:19*

HE HEALED THEM ALL! What a statement, and
what a truth! I praise you and exalt the name of Jesus,

because Jesus and His name are one, Father! There was so much power in His very being, His Presence, that the ever-present virtue flowed out of Him, healing every person. I bless you because you have given me the same power and the authority to use the name of Jesus to let healing virtue flow out of me. I praise you that Jesus was victorious in all circumstances and at all times, therefore because I am a joint-heir with Him, I am victorious and triumphant at all times because of that name! JESUS! Name above all names! I say it out loud!

Apr. 5 *"And in that day you will ask Me nothing. Most assuredly, I say to you, whatever you ask the Father in My name He will give you. Until now you have asked nothing in My name. Ask, and you will receive, that your joy may be full." John 16:23,24*

Your goodness is almost impossible to believe! My joy is full and running all over the place! I thank you, Father, that Jesus said WHATEVER I ask in His NAME, you will give to me. I rejoice and give thanks that the name Jesus has such power and authority. I'm blessed to ask in the name of Jesus because of the love that fills my heart when His name is on my lips and because of the sweet expectation of receiving what I ask from you, Father. Thank you for giving so bountifully in my life that my joy is running over!

Apr. 6 *"You did not choose Me, but I chose you and appointed you that you should go and bear fruit, and that your fruit should remain, that whatever you ask the Father in My name He may give you." John 15:16*

You chose me! You ordained me! You picked me out because you wanted to! I thank you, Father, that I am chosen and ordained through Jesus Christ to bear fruit in my life from the love and truth He expresses in me. Thank you that I live so that people can see the love of Jesus in me and that I can reach out to tell the Good News to others. Thank you that I am appointed to bring forth fruit and that my fruit will remain as your Word says, so that I can ask for anything in Jesus' name and you will give it to me!

Apr. 7   *"Most assuredly, I say to you, he who believes in Me, the works that I do he will do also; and greater works than these he will do, because I go to My Father. And whatever you ask in My name, that I will do, that the Father may be glorified in the Son. If you ask anything in My name, I will do it."* **John 14:12-14**

I believe in you, I do believe on you! I get so excited when I read that I can do even greater things than Jesus did. My mind can't comprehend all the things you've promised, but Father, I believe them because you have said so in your Word. I bless you that your Word makes such a complete and total statement when you picked the word "whatsoever" I asked in the name of Jesus would be done! I want to glorify your Son Jesus in all that I do! I'm walking in power because you said so!

Apr. 8   *"Then Peter said to them, 'Repent, and let every one of you be baptized in the name of Jesus Christ for the remission of sins; and you shall receive the gift of the Holy Spirit.'"* **Acts 2:38**

Father, I rejoice and thank you for the power that's in the name of Jesus! I thank you that at that name the lame shall walk, the blind shall see, and healings shall take place today just as they did in the days when the disciples walked on this earth. I thank you for the blessings that the name of Jesus brings. Thank you for the gift of the Holy Spirit. Thank you for the power that comes with the Holy Spirit. Thank you for the joy that comes with the Holy Spirit. I praise you, Father, that you give ALL of your blessings to ALL of your children. I'm not going to miss a single one!

Apr. 9   *"And these signs will follow those who believe: In My name they will cast out demons; they will speak with new tongues."* **Mark 16:17**

Glorious Father, how I praise and thank you that in the NAME of Jesus I have power over devils. They all know who He is, and I don't have to fear them one bit because the devil himself trembles at the very name of Jesus! Thank you, Father, that all the powers of darkness are afraid and run away at the mention of Jesus, because through Him, they and their deceptions and sneaky, evil plans are defeated. What a blessing you give to us Jesus, when we speak with new tongues. Thank you, Father, for the language of love you give us with which to praise you and love you. Thank you that this is for all believers, and that includes ME! Thank you for these two signs!

Apr. 10   *". . .they will take up serpents; and if they drink anything deadly, it will by no means hurt them; they will lay hands on the sick, and they will recover." Mark 16:18*

Thank you, Father, that as I look at my hands I don't see anything powerful. I don't see anything unusual, I don't see much of anything except fingers on each hand. But your Word says that in the NAME of Jesus, these ordinary hands can be laid on sick people and THEY WILL RECOVER! I praise you for not saying maybe, or that only some would be used, but you just simply said that the hands of believers would be used! I'm a believer, Father, and even though I might not be able to feel power flowing through my hands at all times, by faith in your Word, I know it's there, and I know that the sick will recover when my hands are laid upon them! Thank you that my family is made whole by the use of my hands!

Apr. 11   *"And they called them and commanded them not to speak at all nor teach in the name of Jesus...saying, 'Did we not strictly command you not to teach in this name? And look, you have filled Jerusalem with your doctrine, and intend to bring this Man's blood on us!' Then Peter and the other apostles answered and said: 'We ought to obey God rather than men.'" Acts 4:18, Acts 5:28,29*

Thank you, Father, that the NAME of Jesus has so much power that the devil and his cohorts flee at the very mention of His name. I thank you that the Sadducees were so afraid of the power at the mention of the name of Jesus that they forbade Peter and John to ever speak of His name. Thank you for their boldness in saying, "We ought to obey God rather than men." I praise you that I can use that same boldness today and say the exact same words that I'm a God-pleaser and not a people-pleaser. Bless you for the power in that name.

Apr. 12 *"Then those who went before and those who followed cried out, saying: 'Hosanna! Blessed is He who comes in the name of the Lord!'" Mark 11:9*

Father, I thank you that I come in the name of the Lord, because I am a child of God, redeemed by the blood of the Lamb, the sacrifice of Jesus Christ on the cross, and because of the word of my testimony. I rejoice and praise you, Father, that because I come in His NAME, I am blessed. Thank you for sending your Son, Jesus, to prepare the way for us to follow Him. Hosanna, I'm singing and shouting His praises because I come in His Name!

Apr. 13 *"Heaven and earth will pass away, but My words will by no means pass away." Matthew 24:35*

Father, it is beyond my comprehension that this earth will some day pass away, and that the sun, moon and stars that I've seen and been used to all my life, will pass away, but I believe it because your Word says so! I rejoice that the things of your eternal kingdom shall not pass away, and that you have chosen me to spend eternity in your glorious kingdom because of my salvation in Jesus Christ! How I thank you for sending your Son to us and how I praise you for giving me your Word to stand on all the days of my life. It lifts my spirit up to the heavenly places when I think of these wonderful promises!

Apr. 14 *"Behold, I give you the authority to trample on ser-pents and scorpions, and over all the power of the enemy, and nothing shall by any means hurt you."* *Luke 10:19*

That is real power, Father! I thank you because Jesus unreservedly gave us the power to walk on snakes and scorpions without harm. I thank you that this power was magnified to give us power over all the enemy, without possibility of retaliation upon us, because Jesus guaranteed that nothing would be able by any means to hurt us. I praise you, Father, be-cause Jesus didn't limit our power to particular con-ditions, and didn't say we only had power over part of the enemy but over ALL the enemy's power! Thank you, Father, that nothing is going to hurt us because Jesus gave us that power in His name!

Apr. 15 *"Assuredly, I say to you, whoever does not receive the kingdom of God as a little child will by no means enter it."* *Luke 18:17*

Glory, Father, I'm so thankful because getting into your kingdom is so simple that I'm going to shout out your praises! What a blessing that I am not required to have a college degree. I don't even have to speak Greek or Hebrew, and I don't have to belong to a certain club or be an expert in anything. I'm so glad that you let me join your special club just by simple faith in the blood of Jesus. I didn't come in by intel-lect or meditation or muscles. There wasn't anything to figure out, I didn't have to buy a ticket, and there was no red tape. How I praise you, Father, that you sent Jesus to show me the way!

Apr. 16 *"But He said, 'The things which are impossible with men are possible with God.'"* *Luke 18:27*

That's the epitome of an impossible statement, Fa-ther, because many times we're limited by what sci-ence says. We've been taught that if science can't solve a problem or heal a disease, it can't be done! I praise you, Father, because there is an infinitely greater hope, an infinitely greater power than science. Because Jesus said it, it's so! Those very things which are impossible with men are possible with you. Thank you, Father, that through you I can expect the impossible and the miraculous to happen! You are the changeless God! You are the same God of miracles today as you were 2,000 years ago, or in Moses' time, or at the creation! Bless you that you are MY Father!

Apr. 17   *"...for the Son of Man has come to seek and to save that which was lost." Luke 19:10*

He searched for me, He hunted me, He pursued me, He sought me! Thank you, Father, for sending your very own Son, Jesus, to rescue me when I was lost in the darkness of sin. I thank you that you loved me so much, you let your own Son bear my sins upon the cross, so that I might be cleansed and saved from eternal damnation. I was lost, but He found me and saved me so I could become part of your kingdom! I rejoice that Jesus shined His light on the path that led me right to your gate! Father, I will praise you and glorify your name forever that your Son was sacrificed so I could have eternal life! Thank you, Father!

Apr. 18   *"...For the joy of the Lord is your strength." Neh. 8:10*

Jesus gives joy! Glory to God, how I sing hosanna to the highest because of the joy which overflows in my heart. I praise you that the redeemed of the Lord shall return and come with singing unto Zion: and everlasting joy shall be upon their heads. How I praise you that they shall obtain gladness and joy, and sorrow and sighing shall flee away. I can rejoice because my name is written in heaven. Father, I thank you for the beautiful words of the angel when he said, "Behold, I bring you good tidings of great joy!" Thank you that the Good News was Jesus and the good tidings still bring joy today. Father, I'm walking and leaping and praising you because of the overabundance of joy in my heart!

Apr. 19 *"Therefore if the Son makes you free, you shall be free indeed." John 8:36*

"Most assuredly, I say to you, if anyone keeps My word he shall never see death." John 8:51

I'm free, I'm free, I'm free, for whom the Son sets free is free indeed! I am liberated, I am unconditionally set free! I am unquestionably set free! Glory, Father, I thank you for the freedom I have in this beautiful country of ours, but I thank you much more for the freedom Jesus came to bring me! Thank you that you sent Jesus to free me from bondage to sin and to free me from death, which your Word says is the wages of sin. I rejoice and praise your name, Father, because now I shall never see spiritual death! I have a glorious eternal life ahead of me, and I'm enjoying it right this very minute! Thank you, Father! Hallelujah!

Apr. 20 *"The thief does not come except to steal, and to kill, and to destroy. I have come that they may have life, and that they may have it more abundantly." John 10:10*

I hate the devil! He's a robber, a crook, a pirate, a burglar, and good for nothing! He steals, he robs, he plunders, he hijacks, he swindles, he blackmails, he cheats, and he tries to destroy everything that comes his way! Father, how I love you that Jesus came to give me the abundant life by restoring me to your love, the source of all abundance! I thank you that the devil who comes as a thief, is powerless to steal the new life I have in you, because he has to run from the very name of Jesus! Thank you, Father, for my new life of abundance – love, joy, health, prosperity, and ETERNAL LIFE IN YOUR KINGDOM! Hallelujah!

Apr. 21 *"Most assuredly, I say to you, unless a grain of wheat falls into the ground and dies, it remains alone; but if it dies, it produces much grain."* **John 12:24**

I see a whole wheatfield, Father, swaying in the breeze of the Holy Spirit. How I thank you that Jesus died on the cross and rose again the third day, to bring forth the fruit of salvation in us so we might have eternal life in your kingdom! I thank you that I'm part of that fruit crop! If that one kernel had not died, Father, there would have never been a way for me to have eternal life. My sins were washed away in the blood of the Lamb you sent as a living sacrifice for me! I rejoice because I'm a new person living a NEW life in your love, and all of this was made possible through one precious kernel – your lovely Son Jesus!

Apr. 22 *"And such were some of you. But you were washed, but you were sanctified, but you were justified in the name of the Lord Jesus and by the Spirit of our God."* *I Corinthians 6:11*

Father, how I praise you that I have been washed absolutely clean and spotless and purified by a complete atonement for sin and made free from the guilt of sin, that I am set apart, consecrated, purified, sanctioned and authorized in that name that is above all names! I praise you that I have been pronounced righteous, and that all the things which you held against me before I was saved, are now just as if they had never happened. I take that wonderful name upon my lips at all times and tell the world about the wonderful things that happen in that Name!

Apr. 23 *"Peace I leave with you, My peace I give to you; not as the world gives do I give to you. Let not your heart be troubled, neither let it be afraid."* **John 14:27**

It certainly is different from the world, Father! I rejoice and thank you for that very special kind of peace that Jesus gave me. I praise you that I don't have to be agitated and disturbed by happenings in the world, because that's not the kind of peace you give. That special peace is a divine peace that calms my heart and mind in exactly the same manner Jesus did when He once commanded a storm to cease when His disciples in the boat became afraid. I praise you, Father, that nothing and no one can ever trouble my heart or take away the peace that Jesus gave me, because it's divine, and it's mine!

Apr. 24 *"If you abide in Me, and My words abide in you, you will ask what you desire, and it shall be done for you." John 15:7*

Jesus, I'm abiding in you! I'm vitally united to you through your Word, and I'm letting your words settle down deep inside of me, into all the dark corners of my life so that they will permanently dwell, reside, live and stay within me at all times. I'm speaking your words, I'm saying your words, I'm living your words, I'm loving your words! I'm blessed and thankful to be always with you and your abiding love, to be able to ask ANYTHING of you and know that it will be done. Father, I praise you and bless you because you are always there to provide answers to my problems, to love me and nourish me and lift me up! I'm soaring higher all the time because I'm abiding in you and you're abiding in me!

Apr. 25 *"To them God willed to make known what are the riches of the glory of this mystery among the Gentiles: which is Christ in you, the hope of glory." Col. 1:27*

Thank you, Father, that you have made known to me what was once a mystery to the Gentiles, because the mystery is simply that Jesus Christ lives right inside me! I praise you because with Jesus inside me, I have the riches of glory, the power to live righteously in this world and the hope of eternal life in your kingdom! Thank you, Father, that it pleases you to make this mystery known to me, so I can live by faith in your grace through Jesus Christ, and let my light shine before mankind! I don't know how He does it, Father, and that's not important! The important thing is that He does!

Apr. 26 *"...and have put on the new man who is renewed in knowledge according to the image of Him who created him... Therefore, as the elect of God, holy and beloved, put on tender mercies, kindness, humbleness of mind, meekness, longsuffering;" Col. 3:10,12*

I'm sparkling, I'm clean, I'm shiny and I'm new! Father, thank you that I am a new person in Christ, with a new spiritual self which is continually renewed and perfected in knowledge, after the image of my Creator. Thank you that I'm being sanctified and made holy as one of your elect, because to do your works I've been given your characteristics - mercy, kindness, humility, meekness, patience, and willingness to endure whatever comes before me. Thank you, Father, for your love, because these things would never be mine in the flesh, but they are mine because of you.

Apr. 27 *"For God did not call us to uncleanness, but in holiness." I Thessalonians 4:7*

I praise you, Father, for your Word which speaks loud and clear, that my calling is not just a part-time job, where I can do your holy work part of the time and fool around with sin at other times. Thank you that YOU WANT ALL OF ME ALL THE TIME! I praise you that I don't have unclean desires and thoughts, because you protect and shield me from the filth that the devil throws at me. Thank you, Father, that as I follow Jesus Christ and abide in Him, the power of righteousness now flows through me, and I am victorious in Christ!

Apr. 28 *"If any of you is deficient in wisdom, let him ask of the giving God [Who gives] to every one liberally and* *ungrudgingly, without reproaching or faultfinding, and it will be given him. Only it must be in faith that he asks, with no wavering - no hesitating, no doubting. For the one who wavers (hesitates, doubts) is like the billowing surge out at sea, that is blown hither and thither and tossed by the wind. " James 1:5,6 Amp.*

Father, I just thank you for all the things I can ask in the NAME of Jesus. Thank you for telling me that if I lack wisdom, all I have to do is ask and it is mine, given liberally without question. I rejoice in the strength of faith I have to ask and receive from you, and I thank you that I'm not blown this way and that way like a weathervane. Thank you, Father, that my faith is steady and constant. I really appreciate the fact that even though I might be very deficient in natural wisdom, because I have asked, I have received divine wisdom because I have the mind of Christ!

Apr. 29 *"Therefore submit to God. Resist the devil and he will flee from you. Draw near to God and He will draw near to you. Cleanse your hands, you sinners; and purify your hearts, you double-minded." James 4:7,8*

Devil, I'm resisting you, so you can't come close to me! Thank you, Father, that I can come before you with clean hands and a pure heart. I submit myself completely to you, giving thanks that as I draw near to you, you come closer and closer to me. I praise you, Father, that I have power not only to resist the devil, but to chase him away completely. He has to flee before your power. No longer will I be double-minded with wavering and divided interests, but I shall be single-minded, desiring only to serve and love you! The devil can't touch me!

Apr. 30 *"For if you remain completely silent at this time, relief and deliverance will arise for the Jews from another place, but you and your father's house will per-*

ish. Yet who knows whether you have come to the kingdom for such a time as this?" Esther 4:14

Father, how we bless you that Jesus came to the world for such a time as this. Thank you that your timing is perfect in all things. We are excited about that day when your perfect timing will close the world as we know it today, and the book will be completed, because we know it will be just right! In the midst of the world's failing economy system, thank you that we stand on that solid rock of Jesus! We glory in your perfect timing!

MAY

BLESSINGS
GOD WANTS YOU TO BE BLESSED!

God loves us so much that His heart cries when we don't avail ourselves of all the blessings He wants to give us. Look how easy He makes it for us: *"Christ has redeemed us from the curse of the law, having become a curse for us (for it is written, 'Cursed is everyone who hangs on a tree'), that the blessing of Abraham might come upon the Gentiles in Christ Jesus, that we might receive the promise of the Spirit through faith... And if you are Christ's, then you are Abraham's seed, and heirs according to the promise"* Galatians 3:13,14,29. Every blessing that belonged to Abraham belongs to you and to me. Hallelujah!

May 1   *"Blessed is the man who walks not in the counsel of the ungodly, nor stands in the path of sinners, nor sits in the seat of the scornful; but his delight is in the law of the Lord, and in His law he meditates day and night. He shall be like a tree planted by the rivers of water, that brings forth its fruit in its season, whose leaf also shall not wither; and whatever he does shall prosper."* **Psalm 1:1-3**

Father, I'm blessed, blessed, blessed! I'm happy, fortunate, and prosperous because I don't follow the advice, plans or purposes of the ungodly. I'm blessed because I'm not inactive where the sinners are concerned. Just lead me to them and I'll share the Good News. I certainly am not going to sit down with the scoffers and mockers, but I constantly meditate in your laws and your words. I bless you that your promises are music to my ears and sweet as honey in my mouth. I thank you that everything I do in you prospers in a marvelous way because my joy is in your law.

May 2   *"The Lord is my shepherd; I shall not want. He makes me to lie down in green pastures; he leads me beside the still waters. He restores my soul; he leads me in the paths of righteousness for His name's sake." Ps. 23:1-3*

I lack nothing in my life, Father, because you lead me to beautiful places where I am nourished and at peace, both physically and spiritually. Father, I praise you and thank you for that, because you are my shepherd, my light and my hope. You feed and clothe me and restore my soul when I'm weary, because you love me as a shepherd loves his flock. I thank you that whenever I'm rushing around too much, you lead me beside the still waters, out of the turmoil of life. Thank you, Father, for protecting me from the wolves of the world and for leading me in the paths of righteousness.

May 3   *"Yea, though I walk through the valley of the shadow of death, I will fear no evil; for you are with me; your rod and your staff, they comfort me. You prepare a table before me in the presence of my enemies;" Ps. 23:4-5*

Father, thank you that I don't walk into the valley of the shadow of death and sit down. No, you've said that I walk THROUGH the deep, sunless valley of the shadow of death. Hallelujah, I'm walking right out of that valley, whether it be sickness, poverty or depression, and I fear or dread no evil because YOU protect me. Thank you for preparing a spiritual feast for me right in front of my enemies! I don't even have to ask them to sit down because they don't have any right to disturb me! They turn their back on spiritual food anyway, but hallelujah, it cures my indigestion!

May 4   *"...You anoint my head with oil; my cup runs over. Surely goodness and mercy shall follow me all the days of my life; and I will dwell in the house of the Lord forever. Ps. 23:5-6*

How I rejoice, Father, that I'm so blessed, because you anoint my head with so much of the oil of the Holy Spirit that my cup runs over. You didn't give me just a little trickle, you gave me a cup that runs and runs and runs over! Thank you, Father, that two things are going to follow me all the days of my life and those are goodness and mercy! Not sorrow and sadness, but goodness and mercy, and I thank you because I'm blessed to be able to dwell in the house of the Lord forever!

May 5   *"Blessed is he whose transgression is forgiven, whose sin is covered." Psalm 32:1*

I'm blessed! I'm happy! I'm fortunate! I'm to be envied! All because my sins are forgiven! My sins are covered by that precious blood in such a way that you can't even see them. I'm walking on air because a huge burden has been lifted from my shoulders and replaced by that wonderful blessing because ALL my sins are gone. I'm walking on air! How I bless you that the blood of Jesus was sufficient to cover the sins of the whole world, including mine, and I praise you that when you forgive sins you also forget them, so that I'm a brand new person to you. How I bless you because of the tremendous and unending supply of love you've poured out on me!

May 6   *"Delight yourself also in the Lord, and He shall give you the desires of your heart. Commit your way to the Lord, trust also in Him, and He shall bring it to pass." Psalm 37:4-5*

I delighted in you and with you, Lord, and my heart is overflowing with good measure. You see deep and directly into my heart and you give me the desires of my heart first of all, because you have taken out those carnal desires of the flesh I once had, and you have replaced them with your divine desires. You even grant those secret requests that no one knows about except you and me. How I praise you because since

I've committed my life to you and trust you completely, you will give me what I desire, the real Grade "A" things, and no Grade "B" substitutes or plastic imitations. No one has a better father than I do, because YOU are my Father, and your promises stagger my wildest imagination. Hallelujah! I'm blessed because you're bringing things to pass! Glory!

May 7   Read the entire 136th Psalm before making the following confession.

Heavenly Father, I'm blessed because you are a good God and your mercy endures forever. I've committed sins that seemed to be unforgivable, but in your mercy you have forgiven them. You've given me a beautiful world in which to live because of your mercy. You have given me friends who delight my heart and you've kept my enemies off my back, because of your mercy. Lord, you didn't have to do any of these things for me - but you did, because of your mercy. Thank you, Father, for your loving kindness and mercy which are not temporary things, but eternal, everlasting blessings because they continue unceasingly and eternally! They never wear out, or go sour, but last forever and forever!

May 8   *"You have hedged me behind and before, and laid Your hand upon me. Such knowledge is too wonderful for me; it is high, I cannot attain it. Where can I go from your Spirit? Or where can I flee from Your presence? If I ascend into heaven, You are there; if I make my bed in hell, behold, You are there. If I take the wings of the morning, and dwell in the uttermost parts of the sea, even there Your hand shall lead me, and Your right hand shall hold me." Psalm 139:5-10*

Father, I'm blessed by your glorious presence wherever I go; whether I'm in Arkansas, New York, Zambia, or China. If I was an astronaut, Father, I'd find you in outer space. I rejoice in the blessing of your presence from which I never want to depart, for it's your hand that guides me along the straight and narrow path. Thank you, Lord, for your presence in my life. Thank you that I can never be lost to your sight!

May 9   *"Blessed be the Lord my Rock, who trains my hands for war, and my fingers for battle - my lovingkindness and my fortress, my high tower and my deliverer, my shield and the One in whom I take refuge, who subdues my people under me." Psalm 144:1,2*

Father, I'm blessed because your keen strength and supreme power protect me under all conditions, no matter how difficult they look. I'm blessed too, because your strength makes me a spiritual warrior, armed with the razor-sharp sword of your righteousness, so that I actively take part in the war against darkness. I'm blessed because you never leave me nor forsake me and your steadfast love surrounds me at all times. You are my high tower of safety, my deliverer, and my shield to protect me from the darts of the devil at all times, and you subdue those enemies who try to attack me! I glory in such a glorious God!

May 10   *"Blessed be the God and Father of our Lord Jesus Christ, who has blessed us with every spiritual blessing in the heavenly places in Christ." Ephesians 1:3*

All spiritual blessings in heavenly places are mine! I give you praise, laudation and eulogy because you are the Father of our Lord Jesus Christ, the Messiah. I rejoice that Jesus is with you in heaven and is preparing a place for me there, because I'm ready for that wonderful day when He will come to get me and take me home to you. In the meantime, I'm going to enjoy all those Holy-Spirit-given blessings in heaven and earth which you've passed on to us through your wonderful Son! Glory!

May 11   *"Christ as redeemed us from the curse of the law, having become a curse for us (for it is written, 'Cursed is everyone who hangs on a tree'), that the blessing of Abraham might come upon the Gentiles in Christ*

Jesus, that we might receive the promise of the Spirit through faith. And if you are Christ's, then you are Abraham's seed, and heirs according to the promise." Galatians 3:13,14,29

I'm redeemed by the blood of the Lamb! I'm free from the curse! Father, I'm so blessed that I've been redeemed from the curse of the law because Jesus Christ was made a curse for me so that the blessings of Abraham might come to me. I thank you for sending the Lord Jesus to wash my sins away and remove the curse that had separated me from you and your love, for your love lifts and blesses me constantly. Thank you, Father, for your endless blessings! Bless you for making me an heir to all the promises of Abraham because I am His seed!

May 12 *"Do not be deceived, God is not mocked; for whatever a man sows, that he will also reap. For he who sows to his flesh will of the flesh reap corruption, but he who sows to the Spirit will of the Spirit reap everlasting life." Galatians 6:7,8*

I'm overcome with blessings today, Father, because you've promised that whatever we sow, we shall reap. I'm sowing a bumper crop of love, joy and peace today, Father. I'm not planting my seed in the infertile soil of the flesh because I don't want to reap corruption but I'm sowing to the spirit to be able to reap life everlasting! I praise you that my life is not down here, but my real life is in heaven with you and Jesus! I'm blessed because you make this all possible for me personally, and how I love you for that!

May 13 *"...and raised us up together, and made us sit together in the heavenly places in Christ Jesus, that in the ages to come He might show the exceeding riches of His grace in His kindness toward us in Christ Jesus. For by grace you have been saved through faith, and that not of yourselves; it is the gift of God, not of works, lest anyone should boast." Ephesians 2:6-9*

Glory to God, you've raised me up, and I'm sitting in heavenly places in Christ Jesus. I love you for that. Thank you, Father, that my salvation is not dependent upon my good works, but is entirely dependent upon your grace, because you so simply said if I would believe in Jesus Christ, His work at Calvary, His blood, and would confess it with my mouth, that I would be saved. Hallelujah, Father, I'm saved and filled with your love! I can't boast about it, either, because you did it all!

May 14   *"...that Christ may dwell in your hearts through faith; that you, being rooted and grounded in love, may be able to comprehend with all the saints what is the width and length and depth and height - to know the love of Christ which passes knowledge; that you may be filled with all the fullness of God." Eph. 3:17-19*

Thank you, Father, for blessing me with the knowledge that Christ lives in my heart because I trust in Him. I thank you for blessing me so much with that tremendous love which is so long, so wide, so high and so deep that I will never really be able to understand the greatness of this love for me. Thank you, Father, for the knowledge that some beautiful day I will be filled all the way up to the top with you! What a promise! I don't deserve it, but I receive it!

May 15   *"Finally, my brethren, be strong in the Lord and in the power of His might. Put on the whole armor of God, that you may be able to stand against the wiles of the devil." Eph. 6:10,11* - read also *Eph. 6:12-17*

I praise you, Father, for blessing me with your strength, and the power of your might! Because you provided my whole armor, it is invincible, unconquerable, unyielding and indomitable! I am blessed because even though I don't wrestle against flesh and blood, but against principalities, against powers, against the rulers of the darkness of this world, and against spiritual wickedness in high places, you have given me your whole armor to wear for protection. With the power of your might going before me, Father, I will always be victorious!

May 16   *"Blessed be the Lord, who has given rest to His people Israel, according to all that He promised. There has not failed one word of all His good promise, which He promised through His servant Moses." I Kings 8:56*

What a blessing it is to serve you, Father, because when the world lies and cheats, and fails to keep its word, you are always right there, fulfilling all of your promises. Thank you that the God of Abraham, Isaac and Jacob knows my name, too! Thank you for being a God of integrity, Father, so that we can be imitators of you and be people of integrity in all of our dealings. Thank you that all of the blessings of Abraham are mine because your Word promises this, and you never fail to keep your promises. Hallelujah, what a God I serve! I'm blessed!

May 17   *"Then God blessed them, and God said to them, 'Be fruitful and multiply; fill the earth and subdue it; have dominion over the fish of the sea, over the birds of the air, and over every living thing that moves on the earth.'" Genesis 1:28*

Father, I'm being overtaken and overcome with blessings again because of your love. I'm blessed, I'm blessed, I'm blessed because I have dominion over the fish of the sea, over the fowl of the air, and all living things! I'm blessed because I can be used to multiply your family. I'm blessed because I am fruitful. I'm blessed because I was made in your likeness. I'm blessed because this blessing was upon both man and woman alike, in whom there is no difference in your sight. Glory!

May 18   *"Arise, walk in the land through its length and its width, for I give it to you." Genesis 13:17*

Father, what blessings you give us. Thank you for the privilege of knowing that all the blessings you bestowed in the beginning have come right down through time to us. Thank you for letting us walk through the length and breadth of the land you have for us, knowing that you will give it to us. Thank you for blessing those who bless me and who confer prosperity or happiness upon me. Thank you that I can be a blessing also to others, by dispensing good to them. Thank you for giving me so much land (or possessions) that I will have too much and can share them with others! How I bless you for all your blessings! I'm walking sideways, forward and backward over the land you give to me!

May 19 *"Jesus Christ is the same yesterday, today, and forever." Hebrews 13:8*

Father, I praise and thank you that your Son alone, among all the constant changes taking place in the world, always remains the same. I thank you that because of this He still saves, heals and delivers. He is the living cornerstone of my life, and I am saved, healed and delivered because He hasn't changed one single bit, and never will! I thank you that when the price of gold escalates and soars to new highs, and drops to new lows as well, that Jesus is exactly the same. Thank you for blessing me with a changeless Jesus as my Savior, my healer, my doorway into your marvelous glorious presence. He is my rock, and forever I can rely on His sameness.

May 20 *"Therefore be patient, brethren, until the coming of the Lord. See how the farmer waits for the precious fruit of the earth, waiting patiently for it until it receives the early and latter rain." James 5:7*

Heavenly Father, thank you for the blessed hope I have in the coming of my Lord Jesus Christ. I'm blessed now, Father, because He lives in my heart, waiting for exactly the chosen day to come to me in

person. Thank you for your Word, Father, which
tells me that Christ is like the farmer who waits for
the seasonal rains to bring His crop to full ripeness
before the harvest time. I praise you, Father, for patiently perfecting me in your love so I'll be joyously
prepared for that great day! Hallelujah!

May 21   *"...having been born again, not of corruptible seed
but incorruptible, through the word of God which
lives and abides forever, because 'All flesh is as grass,
and all the glory of man as the flower of the grass.
The grass withers, and its flower falls away, but the
word of the Lord endures forever.'" I Peter 1:23-25*

Glory, Father, I'm born again and glad of it! The
incorruptible seed of your Word has been planted in
my heart and is growing every day! I praise you,
Father, that although the things of this world come
and go, your Word endures forever, a priceless eternal treasure. Thank you for the blessing of your Word!
You are not temporary, you are eternal and everlasting, never wearing out!

May 22   *"For God so loved the world that He gave His only
begotten Son, that whoever believes in Him should
not perish but have everlasting life." John 3:16*

Thank you, Father, that because of your love I can
answer my telephone and say, "God loves you!" and
feel your love going right through that telephone to
the person on the other end. Thank you, Father, that
you love us so much because it's this love that makes
your blessings available to us. Thank you that I am
blessed because you loved me enough to send your
only begotten Son, Jesus, to die for me so that I might
have eternal life! I love you, Father! I believe, I believe, I believe!

May 23   *"But you are a chosen generation, a royal priesthood, a holy nation, His own special people, that you
may proclaim the praises of Him who called you out*

of darkness into His marvelous light;" I Peter 2:9

I'm glad I'm different and unique! I'm blessed to belong to a chosen race, a royal priesthood, a dedicated nation, a member of your own purchased, special people so that I can set forth and show to all the world your wonderful deeds and display the virtues and perfections of your divine nature because you have implanted it in me to minister to the spiritual needs of those around me. I rejoice that I belong to this peculiar race of people because my Lord is King of kings and Lord of lords, who has the power to call whosoever He will out of the darkness and death, into the marvelous light of new life. Thank you, Father, for giving me the blessing of Jesus and your love in Him. I'm peculiar, and I want the world to know the reason for it! Hallelujah!

May 24   *"For the eyes of the Lord are on the righteous, and his ears are open to their prayers; but the face of the Lord is against those who do evil." I Peter 3:12*

Hallelujah, I can't hide from you, Father. I'm so blessed that your eyes are upon the righteous, those who are in right standing with you, because your Word says that you are attentive and sensitive to my prayers. I'm blessed because your ears are open to me 24 hours a day. How I praise you for never tiring of listening to me. Thank you that I am never lost to your sight, but under your tender, loving care at all times. How I praise you that you differentiate between the evil and the righteous, because I would never want to have you turn your face from me! I'm never going to even try to hide from you!

May 25   *"And whatever we ask we receive from Him, because we keep His commandments and do those things that are pleasing in His sight." I John 3:22*

Whatsoever I ask is mine! Glory, what a promise, Father! I'm blessed, Father, because you've given me instructions for life that are written down in a book that I can refer to constantly, and because you shower me with so much love that I rejoice to obey everything you tell me to do! You bless me with your faithfulness, so I bless you with mine! I watchfully and carefully obey all your instructions and do the things that are pleasing in your sight. I observe your suggestions and constantly practice what is pleasing to you, so I thank you for being willing to do whatsoever I ask, because my wishes are in line with what you want for me! Glory, I'm swimming in blessings!

May 26   *"There is no fear in love; but perfect love casts out fear, because fear involves torment. But he who fears has not been made perfect in love." I John 4:18*

Father, I'm blessed that I have no fear in me whatsoever, because I'm protected by your power and strength from all the things of the devil. By your Word, I have no fear in me, and dread does not exist, because your full-blown, perfect love turns fear out-of-doors and gets rid of every trace of terror. I'm blessed, Father, and I praise you that I'm not suffering the torment of darkness, because you've lifted me into the wonderful light and complete perfection of your love. Thank you, Father, for blessing me! Regardless of the circumstances, your love overcomes all fear!

May 27   *"Are they not all ministering spirits sent forth to minister for those who will inherit salvation?" Heb. 1:14*

Thank you, Father, for sending out your angels who are ministering for us constantly because we are heirs of salvation. Thank you, Father, for blessing us with the knowledge that those same angels are out there bringing our loved ones to that person who will minister salvation to them. Thank you that you send angels forth even without my knowing about it, except believing they are there! Thank you for letting them minister for my protection in times of trouble. Thank you because they keep my foot from slipping when the path gets dangerous. Thank you that they could even pet a lion and close his mouth without danger to a child of God. I'm blessed because of angels!

May 28 *"...that the God of our Lord Jesus Christ, the Father of glory, may give to you the spirit of wisdom and revelation in the knowledge of Him, the eyes of your understanding being enlightened; that you may know what is the hope of His calling, what are the riches of the glory of His inheritance in the saints..." Eph. 1:17-18*

Glory, Father, your blessings are overwhelming me with joy because you have granted me a spirit of wisdom, revelation and insight into mysteries and secrets in the deep and intimate knowledge of your Son, because you have flooded the eyes of my heart with light, giving me the privilege of understanding what is the hope of my calling and the riches that are the glorious inheritance of your set-apart ones! I'm blessed because of the magnitude of your blessings!

May 29 *"For you know the grace of our Lord Jesus Christ, that though He was rich, yet for your sakes He became poor, that you through His poverty might become rich." II Corinthians 8:9*

Father, your blessings stagger my imagination! When I think about the fact that Jesus had everything in your kingdom with all its riches and glories for Himself, yet He chose to become poor for my sake, that I could become rich in you, I am overwhelmed! I praise you that I have been delivered from the curse through Him. I bless you that I am saved through grace, because there is no way I could have earned the gift Jesus gave me. It was His kindness and His gracious generosity that make this all possible. I thank you that because of His poverty I have become enriched and abundantly supplied at all times! I thank you that I am progressively becoming acquainted with these blessings more and more all the time!

May 30   *"...while we do not look at the things which are seen, but at the things which are not seen. For the things which are seen are temporary, but the things which are not seen are eternal." II Corinthians 4:18*

Thank you, Father, for giving me spiritual eyes so that I don't have to look and see things the way the world sees them but I can look at them through your eyes. Thank you that I don't have to see only the things which are visible to our human eyes, but I can see with my spiritual eyes the glorious things of your kingdom, which is my inheritance. I praise you for this great blessing! I bless you because even though I've never seen you, I KNOW you're there at all times, loving and protecting me.

May 31   *"Don't let others spoil your faith and joy with their philosophies, their wrong and shallow answers built on men's thoughts and ideas, instead of on what Christ has said. For in Christ there is all of God in a human body; so you have everything when you have Christ, and you are filled with God through your union with Christ. He is the highest Ruler, with authority over every other power." Colossians 2:8,9 TLB*

I HAVE EVERYTHING! Father, what an overwhelming thought to know that I am in Christ and He is in me, because all the treasures of divine wisdom and all the riches of spiritual knowledge and enlightenment are stored up and lie hidden in Him, but they are mine, and I have everything because I am joined with Jesus Christ in salvation. Father, the world can't talk me out of what your Word says is mine! My joy and my faith are at an all-time high, because they stand on what Christ has said. I don't look to the world for their shallow answers and intellectualism, but I look to the Holy Spirit world for my answers to life. Bless you, Father, that you tell us with no qualms that Jesus is the highest ruler! Not only that, He is mine! Hallelujah, therefore I have everything I need in Christ Jesus!

JUNE
LOVE

LOVE is our confession for the month, and what an appropriate subject for the month of June when people think of love and marriage. The love of God for man, and man for God, is the most beautiful love in all the world, because it is this love that makes us lovable to the world, and makes it possible for us to love them. God loves to hear you tell Him how much you love Him, so say it every day, will you?

On June 11th we have asked you to pick out someone to love in a special way. Write and tell us what happened to you and to them, because of this special day of giving love!

If you want to see some problems disappear in a hurry, write all the problems you have on a piece of paper, and at the bottom write: "...In ALL these things we are more than conquerors through him who loved us" Romans 8:37. Confess it every day until you discover that every single one of those problems is conquered!

June 1   *"As the Father loved Me, I also have loved you; abide in My love. If you keep My commandments, you will abide in My love, just as I have kept My Father's commandments and abide in His love. These things I have spoken to you, that My joy may remain in you, and that your joy may be full." John 15:9-11*

My joy is running over and spilling all over the place! Thank you, Father, that in the same way you loved Jesus, He has also loved me. Thank you, Jesus, that because I keep your commandments, I abide in your love all the time. I thank you that I can abide in your love 24 hours a day, because your source never runs out and is always available to me. Thank you that my joy is full and running over. Thank you that you gave your joy, not as a temporary thing, but as a permanent full-time gift, so that your joy and happiness and excitement remains in me and is full and complete and overflowing at all times.

June 2   *"Jesus answered and said to him, 'If anyone loves Me, he will keep My word; and My Father will love him, and We will come to him and make Our home with him.'" John 14:23*

Jesus, I love you, I love you, I love you! Father, thank you that your Son is so lovable. Thank you that I can love Him at all times and keep His words, because His words are true and right and holy! Thank you, Jesus, for giving me words that last forever and never change. How I praise you because you have come to live in me and make your abode in me! Because your love fills me to overflowing, I can love others, not just neighbors, but even enemies! I love you for being so close to me at all times! I thank you that your house is my house and my house is your house!

June 3   *"But as it is written: 'Eye has not seen, nor ear heard, nor have entered into the heart of man the things which God has prepared for those who love Him.'" I Cor. 2:9*

I'm excited today, because I can hardly wait to hear what you're telling me! I praise you, Father, that regardless of whether or not I have 20/20 vision, my eyes have not seen, nor are they capable of seeing all the love that you have for me. Thank you that regardless of how good my hearing is, my ears will never be able to hear all the wonderful truths that you have ready for me. My heart belongs to you, Father, and I'm rejoicing right now because I know you'll have something beautiful beyond words to put in it! Thank you that all these wonderful gifts are especially for me because you love me!

June 4   *"But God demonstrates His own love toward us, in that while we were still sinners, Christ died for us." Romans 5:8*

I was the worst of them all, and yet you still loved me! Thank you, Father, that you loved me in spite of what I was! You didn't look at my faults and failures, but you looked at what you wanted to see in me! How I praise you, Father, that you let your Son die because your love for me was so great that you were willing to let His blood be shed to save me. I receive your love and enjoy it every day because I remember what that love was willing to do! It thrills me when I realize that I didn't have to clean myself up in order to have Jesus willing to die for me; He was willing to do it when I was a miserable character!

June 5 *"Nevertheless the Lord your God would not listen to Balaam, but the Lord your God turned the curse into a blessing for you, because the Lord your God loves you." Deut. 23:5*

Father, how I praise you that you wouldn't listen to Balaam even when He was willing to curse Israel for money, but because you loved your people so much, you were willing to turn the curse into a blessing each time He opened His mouth. Thank you, Father, that the love which reached your people back in the Old Testament times, still reaches me today. I love you for that, Father. I thank you that when my mouth gets out of line, Father, and begins to say the wrong things that don't glorify you, you can still turn my words around, too, to be a blessing to others!

June 6 *"He who has My commandments and keeps them, it is he who loves Me. And he who loves Me will be loved by My Father, and I will love him and manifest Myself to him." John 14:21*

I praise you, Father, that Jesus has given us commandments to keep, because these make the Christian life so simple and straightforward to live; all we have to do is what you tell us to do, and refrain from doing the things you tell us not to do, and we're blessed and living in your love right now. How we praise

you, Jesus, that you have promised to manifest yourself to us because we love you. You've said that you
will let yourself be clearly seen and make yourself
real to me at all times. I really love you!

June 7   *"He who does not love does not know God, for God
is love." I John 4:8*

Father, thank you that your Word tells me the greatest commandment is to love you with every fiber of
my being, and the second is to love my neighbor as
myself. I obey these commandments so that you will
live in my heart and fill me up with even more love!
I praise you because when you created me, you made
me able to receive and to give love, for you are love,
and the river of your love flows continually to your
people! I rejoice in your love, Father, and I thank
you for letting us know in no uncertain terms that
there is plenty of love for all those who open their
hearts to receive it! I love you, Father!

June 8   *"Beloved, if God so loved us, we also ought to love
one another." I John 4:11*

Thank you, Father, for showing us that you love us so
much that there just isn't any excuse for us not loving
one another! Thank you for giving me a soft heart and
the ability to love all my brothers and sisters on this
earth. I know I could never do this on my own but it's
so wonderful to know that because you could love me
through all my sin, all my faults and all my failures, you
can give me the ability to love even those people who
seem unlovable! Thank you, Father, for your Word
teaches that everybody deserves love!

June 9   *"And we have known and believed the love that God
has for us. God is love, and he who abides in love
abides in God, and God in him." I John 4:16*

I glorify your name, Father, because I know and believe how much you love me. You washed my sin
away with the blood of Jesus and there just isn't any

way I can imagine a greater love than that, and there isn't any way I can thank you enough for what you did. But, Father, I want to try - by loving you with everything I've got and by obeying you in all things. I thank you, Father, that I dwell in love because of your love for me, and because of the power of your love, I live in you and you live in me.

June 10 *"This is My commandment, that you love one another as I have loved you. Greater love has no one than this, than to lay down one's life for his friends." John 15:12,13*

Love is the greatest force in the world, Lord Jesus, and is the most powerful word in the Bible except God and Christ Jesus, so I thank you for commanding me to love others in the same way that you loved me. Thank you, that you not only gave your life for your friends, but you gave it for me even though I was an enemy for so many years. How I praise you for showing me the way to love others! I will express your love in me to those I meet, even to those who are hard to love.

June 11 *"And you shall love the Lord your God with all your heart, with all your soul, with all your mind, and with all your strength. This is the first commandment." Mark 12:30*

Father, I love you with all my mind, my heart, my strength and my soul! Because you love me so much, it's easy to love you in return. I worship you, Father, because your first commandment concerns love, which is what everyone in the world needs and deserves. Thank you that in loving you, I receive the power to love everyone. I will find a specific individual to love today. I will concentrate on finding a person who needs love, someone who does not have many friends, and whose heart is crying out for love. I'm going to love that person today with your special love.

June 12 *"A new commandment I give to you, that you love one another; as I have loved you, that you also love one another." John 13:34*

Thank you, Father, that Jesus gave us a new commandment. I praise you that people know we are His disciples because we love in a new way - we love one another AS HE LOVED US! Thank you that Jesus loved us enough to teach us, heal us, and save us from sin by even dying for us! Thank you that this is your limitless love flowing through me right now, a powerful love that enables me to love everyone even as Jesus did. Thank you, Father, that when I obey this commandment to love others, I am at the same time loving you with all my heart, my soul, my mind and my strength.

June 13 *"And I pray that Christ will be more and more at home in your hearts, living within you as you trust in him. May your roots go down deep into the soil of God's marvelous love; and may you be able to feel and understand, as all God's children should, how long, how wide, how deep, and how high his love really is; and to experience this love for yourselves, though it is so great that you will never see the end of it or fully know or understand it. And so at last you will be filled up with God himself." Eph.3:17-19 TLB*

Jesus, be more and more at home in my heart! Father, I praise you that Jesus lives in me! Thank you that my roots are going all the way down deep into your soil, which enables me to feel the tremendous depth of your love for me, even though I know I will never be able to comprehend it with my limited mind. Father, I'm so excited because you promise that some day I will be filled all the way up to the top with you! Glory!

June 14 *"I have given them the glory you gave me - the glorious unity of being one, as we are - I in them and you in me, all being perfected into one - so that the world will know you sent me and will understand that you love them as much as you love me." Jn. 17:22-23 TLB*

Father, I love you, I love you, I love you for so many different reasons but especially for the glorious perfect unity we have in Christ Jesus. He lives in us and you live in Him, and we're all perfected into one glorious body. Father, how you could ever love me as much as you love Jesus is beyond my human comprehension, but I praise you that you do love me just as much as you do Jesus!

June 15 *"But Ruth said: 'Entreat me not to leave you, or to turn back from following after you; for wherever you go, I will go; and wherever you lodge, I will lodge; your people shall be my people, and your God, my God. Where you die, I will die, and there will I be buried. The Lord do so to me, and more also, if anything but death parts you and me.'" Ruth 1:16,17*

Thank you, Father, that this can apply to marriage, and thank you for giving to each married couple the most beautiful words to say to each other which can be said. How we bless you, Father, for encouraging us to stay together in marriage at all times. Thank you for the sacredness of human love as well as divine love, and for allowing us to love our mates in greater ways because of your love pouring through us. I bless you that my place is beside my mate at all times. Bless you for making these words available to all.

June 16 *"There is no fear in love; but perfect love casts out fear, because fear involves torment. But he who fears has not been made perfect in love." I John 4:18*

Thank you, Father, that your perfect, complete, full-grown, faultless love turns fear out-of-doors and gets rid of every trace of terror. I glory in the knowledge that the devil can't touch me with fear, because your love is so complete and surrounds me like a glove and safely wraps me in a love cocoon. I praise you, Father, for letting us grow into love's complete perfection because of your great love for us. Thank you for a love which is without a blemish and unparalleled in human understanding, but which is mine because I belong to you. I love you, Father!

June 17 *"He who loves father or mother more than Me is not worthy of Me. And he who loves son or daughter more than Me is not worthy of Me." Matthew 10:37*

Father, I love you more than anything in the whole wide world! I praise you, Father, because you command and demand that we love you more than our mother or father, or even our children. Thank you for always knowing what is best for us because in giving you first place in our lives and loving you most, you've given us the opportunity to love our own families even more because of your love flowing through us. Thank you for giving me the desire and the ability to love you more than my family and to cling steadfastly to you and walk in your ways. Bless you, Father, because the love of my family is based on you, and not on my own desires. You have first place in my heart!

June 18 *"And walk in love, as Christ also has loved us and given Himself for us, an offering and a sacrifice to God for a sweet-smelling aroma." Ephesians 5:2*

Father, I'm walking in love! I'm running in love! I'm leaping in love and I'm falling in love with Jesus! Thank you for loving us so much and giving us someone so lovable. I'm walking down streets with love, letting it ooze out over the people who don't even like me. I'm talking in love to everyone I meet, including those who try to cheat me! I'm thinking in love, even when my thoughts might be trying to go in other directions. I'm a lover because you've put love into my heart!

June 19 *"Therefore I say to you, her sins, which are many, are forgiven, for she loved much. But to whom little is forgiven, the same loves little." Luke 7:47*

Father, thank you that I can say like Paul that I was the worst of the sinners, and because you forgave so much, it's so easy for me to love you wholeheartedly, without any reservations whatsoever. I love you, Father, because you didn't have just a little to forgive in me; you had a lot, but I thank you that you forgave everything you might have ever held against me, so I love you much, much, MUCH! I bless you because as a result of your forgiveness I walk in peace and in freedom from all the problems that are the result of sin! No wonder I love you so much!

June 20 *"Don't be teamed with those who do not love the Lord, for what do the people of God have in common with the people of sin? How can light live with darkness?" II Corinthians 6:14 TLB*

Lord, I love you so much because you tell us exactly how to find favor in your eyes. Thank you for telling us that we're not to team up with people who don't love you, because that inner being of ours tells us that we don't have anything in common with them. We praise you that you say so simply and effectively that just as darkness and light don't go together, neither do God and sin. Thank you, Lord, that we walk in the light! Thank you for saving us from mismatched alliances in marriage, in business, and in friendship. There's no way a partnership can work with you on one side and the devil on the other. Thank you for pointing it out to me so vividly to keep me from falling into dangerous places again!

June 21 *"Instead, be kind to each other, tenderhearted, forgiving one another, just as God has forgiven you because you belong to Christ." Ephesians 4:32 TLB*

Father, thank you for giving me the power to forgive those who have sinned against me, and I praise you for telling me to be kind, tenderhearted, compassionate and understanding in the same way that you are because I belong to Christ. I love you, Jesus, for living in and through me, which gives me the power and the desire to forgive each and every person who may have ever hurt me. Father, I praise you that I don't have to keep those little hurts in my memory because of your love. Thank you that I can do this quickly, readily and freely because that's the way you forgave me.

June 22 *"Don't just pretend that you love others: really love them. Hate what is wrong. Stand on the side of the good. Love each other with brotherly affection and take delight in honoring each other. Never be lazy in your work but serve the Lord enthusiastically." Romans 12:9-11 TLB*

Devil, I hate you! Father, I love you for putting in my heart such a dislike for the things of the devil, and for allowing me to hate that which is wrong. Thank you that I can stand for the good in this world! Father, I'm so appreciative of the fact that I can live in a world which says "dog eat dog" and yet we can sincerely love each other with brotherly affection because of you. I adore you; and I hate and loathe everything that is evil or ungodly, and I turn in absolute horror from wickedness! Years ago I loved wickedness, and I thank you for delivering me from that love!

June 23 *"If you love your neighbors as much as you love yourself you will not want to harm or cheat him, or kill him or steal from him. And you won't sin with his wife or want what is his, or do anything else the Ten Commandments say is wrong. All ten are wrapped up in this one, to love your neighbor as you love yourself." Romans 13:9 TLB*

I love you, Father, because you give me the power to live the way you want me to, without wanting to harm or cheat my neighbors, nor steal from them. Thank you, Father, that you have wrapped up very neatly all the commandments in this one statement, to love your neighbor as yourself. Thank you, Father, that I can love my neighbors because of you.

June 24 *"For do I now persuade men, or God? Or do I seek to please men? For if I still pleased men, I would not be a servant of Christ." **Galatians 1:10***

I praise your holy name, Father, because you haven't called me to be a people pleaser, but a "God" pleaser. Thank you, Father, that my thoughts can be turned toward you at all times, so that I can think about pleasing you, and being a servant of Jesus Christ. I thank you for allowing me to be at the beck and call of Jesus, to always do His bidding! Glory! I don't have to go along with the crowd and do things I don't want to do because I'm afraid of what they might think about me! I'm your willing, happy and contented servant!

June 25 *"...to speak evil of no one. . ." **Titus 3:2***

Father, let the words of my mouth be acceptable in thy sight! Let me be filled with so much of your love that my tongue will only have words that are sweet as honey. I will bridle my tongue and let no words that are harmful, hurtful, injurious, malignant, disastrous or ruinous come out of my mouth, but my lips shall speak words of love which will bring strength, hope and cheer to someone. I will not gossip or criticize, complain or manufacture untruths about anyone, but will keep my conversation full of your love!

June 26 *"...fulfill my joy by being like-minded, having the same love, being of one accord, of one mind." **Phil. 2:2***

Father, I am filling up with your love so my joy can be complete by living in harmony and being of the same mind and one in purpose, so that I will have the same love for all my brothers and sisters in Christ that I have for only some. I am working toward a unity with people of all denominations, so that strife, selfishness and contentiousness will be ended. I will love those whose doctrines do not exactly agree with mine, if they love Jesus, because if we are like-minded

in that area, we can be in one accord and one mind.
Let the little unimportant things fall by the wayside
and let us dwell on the things which last. Thank you
for giving me a love that is big enough to encompass
doctrinal differences. I'm running over with love! It's
splashing over on everyone I run into and it's blessing each one it falls on because it's your love!

June 27 *"Love is very patient and kind, never jealous or envi-*
ous, never boastful or proud, never haughty or selfish
or rude. Love does not demand its own way. It is not
irritable or touchy. It does not hold grudges and will
hardly even notice when others do it wrong." I Cor.
13:4-5 TLB

Father, thank you for the "love" chapter in the Bible.
Thank you for telling us exactly what love is. Lord,
we love you because you tell us if we're jealous or
envious, then we don't have love. Thank you that
when your wonderful love is flowing through us to
reach others, it will never be irritable or touchy. Thank
you, Father, that this is only possible because of your
love! I praise you that I don't have to insist on my
"rights" and having my own way. How I bless you
that I lost my grudges at the altar of salvation!

June 28 *"There are three things that remain - faith, hope, and*
love - and the greatest of these is love." I Corinthians
13:13 TLB

I praise you, Father, for the three wonderful things
that remain: faith, hope and love. Thank you that the
greatest one of these is love, because without love it
would be difficult to have faith and hope, but with
your love, because it is the greatest of all, we also
have faith and hope. Faith in the knowledge that Jesus
Christ is coming back, and hope that it is going to be
soon. We love you because of the joyful and confident expectation we have of eternal salvation. Thank
you that you enable us to have true affection and love
for you and for our fellow man!

June 29   *"Now hope does not disappoint, because the love of God has been poured out in our hearts by the Holy Spirit who was given to us." Romans 5:5*

Father, I thank you because the love which is in my heart is not a human love I have to generate and work up. I can spread your love all over the world because the special love which is freely given to others has been given to us by you. It isn't anything I had to work for, or beg for, but just one of those beautiful gifts you give to your children. Thank you, Father, that the world can see your love in me. I praise you that I don't have to have unbelief or distrust which would cause me to waver about whether or not I could really love someone, because I am empowered by my faith in you and your promises!

June 30   *"...In ALL these things we are more than conquerors through Him who loved us." Romans 8:37*

Glory to God, I'm more than a conqueror! Father, how I praise you for that word ALL! Thank you for letting me know that I win ALL the battles because of your love. It was that same love that allowed Jesus Christ to die on a cross for me that makes me more than a conqueror in ALL areas of my life. Thank you, that I don't have to bow to the devil in any area, because you've said in ALL these things we are more than conquerors through Him who loved us. Thank you, Father, for another month of victory in Jesus! Thank you that I always have a surpassing victory in everything because of your great love!

July

Freedom From Fear

As we wrote the confessions on fear, we felt a tremendous witness in our spirits that thousands of people are going to be delivered from the bondage of fear, and totally and completely liberated by confessing what God's Words says about fear.

July 1   *". . .Be strong and courageous and get to work. Don't be frightened by the size of the task, for the Lord my God is with you; he will not forsake you. He will see to it that everything is finished correctly." I Chronicles 28:20 TLB*

Today I'm strong and courageous and afraid of nothing! Thank you, Father, that you care for every little detail of my life. I am not frightened by the size of any task because you are always with me. And how I praise you, Father, that you always see to it that every job I do is completed correctly. Thank you that I don't have to live the Christian life in my own strength, but that I can rest in you and be strengthened and assured that the work I do turns out right because you are backing me up all the way!

July 2   *"The wicked flee when no one pursues, but the righteous are bold as a lion." Proverbs 28:1*

Today I am bold, bold, BOLD! Father, I praise you for giving me the boldness of a lion! Thank you that because my righteousness comes from you, I act and make decisions with the courage that comes from knowing you are with me in all I do. Thank you, Father, that I stand up and boldly face all that comes before me in life in a way that the wicked can't imitate because of their fear that the wicked things they've done will catch up with them and destroy them. I praise you that I don't have to always be looking over my shoulder in fear as the wicked do. I get so excited, Father, when I realize I'm always on the winning side! I can charge right into any situation of the devil's making, and the wicked will flee before me because you've made me bold as a lion!

July 3   *"For God has not given us a spirit of fear, but of power and of love and of a sound mind." II Tim. 1:7*

I have a sound mind at all times, because I have the mind of Christ! I love you, praise you, thank you and bless you, Father, because you haven't given me a spirit of fear. I rejoice that fear is never from you but is always from the devil. Because you have given me power over the devil and all his doings, I can boldly dismiss any thoughts or feelings of fear that come before me. Thank you, Father, that you've given me a sound mind and the power to face any situation and be victorious in it!

July 4   *"The thief does not come except to steal, and to kill, and to destroy. I have come that they may have life, and that they may have it more abundantly." John 10:10*

Father, I praise you for the day you granted freedom to our nation. But more than that, I thank you for the freedom and abundance of life you have granted me through your Son, Jesus Christ, who came to defeat the devil and all the devil's evil destructive ways. Thank you, Father, that Jesus came to free us from the bondage of the devil's fear, so that the devil can never again steal the blessings of life from your children, like the thief he really is! Thank you that Jesus is the way, the truth and the life and that through Him I have the abundant life you want all your children to have!

July 5   *"Behold, I give you the authority to trample on serpents and scorpions, and over all the power of the enemy, and nothing shall by any means hurt you." Luke 10:19*

Thank you, Father, that you have given me the power to tread on all the works of the devil without the slightest possibility that any harm can come to me! I rejoice that you've turned the tables on the devil, because now I have power over ALL THE POWER OF THE ENEMY, and he has to run from me! I praise you for making me immune to the enemy's poison stings and fangs because I am triumphant in times of trouble and at peace in the midst of strife. Thank you, Father, for making me a spiritual warrior so I can stomp on the works of the enemy wherever I find them!

July 6   *"Roll your works upon the Lord commit and trust them wholly to Him; [He will cause your thoughts to become agreeable to His will, and] so shall your plans be established and succeed." Proverbs 16:3 Amp.*

Father, I feel like I'm in a big bowling alley, and I've just rolled all my cares, worries and defeats up into one big ball, and I'm rolling them all down the alley right into your arms! I'm committing them to you and trusting them wholly to you and I'm not worrying about them any more! I thank you that my thoughts are all becoming agreeable to your will, and that nothing that comes to my mind will be unpleasing to you, because I'm turning my back on all the lusts of the flesh, and rolling all of my works upon you. I'm excited because I now have total and complete assurance that everything I do is going to be established and succeed. How I praise you that you make no plans for failure in your Word!

July 7   *"The Lord is my shepherd; I shall not want. He makes me to lie down in green pastures; he leads me beside the still waters." Psalm 23:1,2*

I love and praise you, Father, because in the abiding love and care you pour upon me, I fear no evil. With you as my shepherd, I'm surrounded by your protective power at all times and I rejoice that I can relax and enjoy your green pastures and still waters, because wherever you lead me, I have complete trust that all my needs are met. I thank you, Father, for seeing to it that I lack nothing. I praise you because I can look to you for everything I need in my life without the slightest worry or fear, for you provide for me in abundance! I bless you, Father!

July 8   *"Be strong and of good courage, do not fear nor be afraid of them; for the Lord your God, He is the One who goes with you. He will not leave you nor forsake you." Deuteronomy 31:6*

Father, I'm strong! I'm courageous! I praise you that I'm not afraid because you are with me in all your power and glory and righteousness and because nothing can withstand your might! I give thanks that you are the Lord my God, who never fails me or leaves me no matter what kind of difficulty or showdown I have to face. You are the strength of my arm and the courage in my heart, so I fear nothing that man can do. Glory, Father, I'm blessed with victory!

July 9   *"The Lord is my light and my salvation; whom shall I fear? The Lord is the strength of my life; of whom shall I be afraid? When the wicked came against me to eat up my flesh, my enemies and foes, they stumbled and fell. Though an army should encamp against me, my heart shall not fear; though war should rise against me, in this I will be confident." Psalm 27:1-3*

I have no fear of anybody or anything! Thank you, Father, for shining your light on the path of righteousness so I can see to walk in your ways. Thank you for saving me from sin and darkness in this life and from eternal damnation in the next, because you love me so much. You are my strength and my shield, Father, so I fear neither the wickedness of my enemies nor the tricks of the devil, because you will cause them to stumble and fall without laying a finger on me. Hallelujah!

July 10   *"For in the time of trouble He shall hide me in His pavilion; in the secret place of His tabernacle He shall hide me; He shall set me high upon a rock." Psalm 27:5*

I rejoice, Father, that you protect and hide me from any kind of trouble that comes my way! Thank you that you always hide me in your pavilion or in the secret of your tabernacle where the wicked dare not follow. How I bless and praise you, Father, that no matter what deceitful lying schemes the devil comes up with to disrupt my life, you'll take me out of harm's way and set me upon a rock where he can't touch me! I love you, Father!

July 11   *"And now my head shall be lifted up above my enemies all around me; therefore I will offer sacrifices of joy in His tabernacle; I will sing, yes, I will sing praises to the Lord." Psalm 27:6*

Father, I praise you because I don't have to look up at my enemies, for you lift my head above them so that I'm looking down on them! You are the God of deliverance and the God of my salvation, Father, and I offer sacrifices of joy to you in celebration of the wonderful way you take care of me! I'm singing praises to you because you lift me above the trials and tribulations of the world and because I love you with all my heart! Glory!

July 12   *"There is therefore now no condemnation to those who are in Christ Jesus, who do not walk according to the flesh, but according to the Spirit. For the law*

*of the Spirit of life in Christ Jesus has made me free
from the law of sin and death." Romans 8:1,2*

How I praise you, Father, that I fear no condemnation
in my life, because there isn't any there! I rejoice because I am in Jesus Christ and I walk after the Spirit!
Thank you for the promises in your Word, for your
Word says that all my sins are forgiven and that you
don't even remember them, so I don't have any fear of
the past. I praise you, Father, that by the law of the
Spirit of life in Jesus, I'm free from the law of sin and
death so that everything before me, everything in my
future, is absolutely wonderful and blessed! Hallelujah!

July 13 *"Have I not commanded you? Be strong and of good
courage; do not be afraid, nor be dismayed, for the
Lord your God is with you wherever you go." Josh. 1:9*

How I thank you, Father, that the power and truth of
your commandment make me strong and fill me with
courage! Fear and dismay have no part in my life,
because my strength is in you, and I trust you in all
things. When the devil comes against me I am brave
and jubilant, for I know you are with me every moment day and night and I have victory over all the
power of darkness! Thank you, Father, that you are
with me wherever I go!

July 14 *"Behold, God is my salvation, I will trust and not be
afraid; for YAH, the Lord, is my strength and my song;
He also has become my salvation. Therefore with joy
you will draw water from the wells of salvation."
Isaiah 12:2,3*

Father, I rejoice that you are my salvation! Because
of this I place my whole trust in you and I am never
afraid or anxious in anything. I rejoice in you because you are my strength and my song, and with so
much confidence and happiness bubbling through me,
I sing your praises everywhere I go! Father, I thank
you for the wells of your salvation, because the liv-

ing water I draw from them renews, blesses and re-
freshes my life and gives me such joy that I feel like
telling everyone I meet what a glorious God you are!

July 15   *"Inasmuch then as the children have partaken of flesh
and blood, He Himself likewise shared in the same,
that through death He might destroy him who had the
power of death, that is, the devil, and release those
who through fear of death were all their lifetime subject to bondage." Hebrews 2:14,15*

Thank you, Father, that Jesus took death upon Himself so He could destroy the one who had the power
of death - the devil. Thank you that I'm free of the
fear of death and free of the desperate hunger for
power, money and the things of this world that come
from fearing death. I praise you, Father, that Jesus
delivered me from sin, the devil and bondage to fear
by shedding His blood for me upon the cross, and I
thank you for that glorious promise of eternal life in
your kingdom! Because death couldn't hold Jesus in
the grave, it won't hold me either, and I'm rejoicing
because my eternal home is in heaven with you! Thank
you, Father, for the priceless blessing of eternal life!

July 16   *"There is no fear in love; but perfect love casts out
fear, because fear involves torment. But he who fears
has not been made perfect in love." I John 4:18*

I praise and thank you, glorious Father, that your
perfect love flows through me in such great measure
that it has cast out fear of any kind and all kinds! I
thank you, Father, for removing the torment of fear
from my life, for torment comes from the devil, and
the devil has to run from the power of your perfect
love! I'm blessed beyond my wildest dreams, Father,
because I'm being perfected in your wonderful love!

July 17   *"God is our refuge and strength, a very present help
in trouble. Therefore we will not fear, though the earth
be removed, and though the mountains be carried*

into the midst of the sea; though its waters roar and be troubled, though the mountains shake with its swelling. Selah." Psalm 46:1-3

Father, I thank you and praise you because you are my refuge and strength, you are my help at the moment trouble comes. I thank you that I don't need to fear even if the world blows up and the mountains crumble into the sea, for you are the God of my salvation and you will take care of me no matter what happens. Father, I praise you because you are the Creator, the God of everything, and for that reason I don't fear anything in the entire universe. Whether the world falls apart or a great earthquake rocks the mountains, I'll be saved and protected by your loving power! Hallelujah!

July 18 *"I am trusting God – oh, praise his promises! I am not afraid of anything mere man can do to me! Yes, praise his promises. I will surely do what I have promised, Lord, and thank you for your help. For you have saved me from death and my feet from slipping, so that I can walk before the Lord in the land of the living." Psalm 56:10-13 TLB*

Glory, Father, I trust you so much that there's no room in my life for fear! I praise your promises, for you always keep them, and I thank you for all the help you've given me. I thank you for saving me from death and for keeping my feet from slipping, so I can walk in your ways. Father, I rejoice in your light!

July 19 *"He who dwells in the secret place of the Most High shall abide under the shadow of the Almighty. I will say of the Lord, 'He is my refuge and my fortress; my God, in Him I will trust.'" Psalm 91:1,2*

I thank you, Father, because I abide in the safety and comfort of your shadow where no evil can touch me. You are my refuge and my fortress, Father, and I thank you and praise you that you are a God who keeps all His promises to His children, so that my trust is always fulfilled in you. Because I dwell in the secret place of the most High, the devil can't make fear fall upon me, but instead I am lifted up and blessed over and over by the love and power with which you surround me!

July 20   *"No evil shall befall you, nor shall any plague come near your dwelling; for He shall give His angels charge over you, to keep you in all your ways." Psalm 91:10,11*

Father, thank you that no evil can befall me and no plague or sickness can come near my house, because you said so! Thank you that I don't have to worry about these things any more, for you've sent your angels and charged them to take care of me in every way! I praise you, Father, for loving me so much that your angels stick by me night and day to guard and protect me and my house and family from everything the devil might try to do to us. Thank you, Father, that your Word frees me from fear of sickness, calamity and disease! Hallelujah!

July 21   *"So he answered and said to me: 'This is the word of the Lord to Zerubbabel: "Not by might nor by power, but by My Spirit," says the Lord of hosts.'" Zechariah 4:6* See also the Amplified Bible.

Praise you, Father, that an angel of the Lord spoke to Zerubbabel and told him that the addition of the bowl to the candlestick caused it to yield a never ending supply of oil from the olive trees. Father, I bless you that oil is the symbol of your Holy Spirit, so its supply continues eternally. Thank you that I don't have to have fear because you've promised that I don't have to win battles in my own strength, nor my own power, but that you will win them for me by your Spirit! Glory! Here I am, winning again!

July 22   *"God blesses those who obey him; happy the man who puts his trust in the Lord." Proverbs 16:20 TLB*

I love to receive your blessings, Father, because I know that everything that comes from you is good! I obey you without hesitation, because everything you tell me to do comes from your righteousness, and I rejoice in your righteousness. I have no fear, nervousness, worry or care about the future or about problems, because your blessings are upon me. I'm happy and I'm singing your praises because I put my trust, my faith, my confidence, and my hope in you. I'm full of anticipation for the good things in life, and fear went out the window when faith and trust came in! Glory!

July 23   *"The Lord by wisdom founded the earth; by understanding He established the heavens; by His knowledge the depths were broken up, and clouds drop down the dew. My son, let them not depart from your eyes – keep sound wisdom and discretion; so they will be life to your soul and grace to your neck. Then you will walk safely in your way, and your foot will not stumble. When you lie down, you will not be afraid; yes, you will lie down and your sleep will be sweet. Do not be afraid of sudden terror, nor of trouble from the wicked when it comes; for the Lord will be your confidence, and will keep your foot from being caught." Proverbs 3:19-26*

Father, I praise and thank you that your wisdom which founded the earth is the same wisdom which guides my life and guards me from fear of falling or of stumbling. You are my confidence, Father, and by your wisdom and knowledge there is life in my soul and grace to my neck. Father, I am awed by the magnificent miracle of your creation, and my sleep is sweet because your children are protected day and night by your mighty power! Hallelujah!

July 24   *"The fear of man brings a snare, but whoever trusts in the Lord shall be safe." Proverbs 29:25*

I thank you, Father, for taking all fear from me, because fear is just an invitation for the devil to take advantage with one of his deceitful snares. I love and praise you, Father, for being the kind of God that I can trust with all my heart, for you are always faithful to keep your children safe and filled with blessings. You are wonderful to me!

July 25 *"But Moses told the people, 'Don't be afraid. Just stand where you are and watch, and you will see the wonderful way the Lord will rescue you today. The Egyptians you are looking at – you will never see them again. The Lord will fight for you, and you won't need to lift a finger.' Then the Lord said to Moses, 'Quit praying and get the people moving! Forward, march!'" Exodus 14:13-15 TLB*

Father, thank you for the simplicity, directness and power of the ways you deliver us from seemingly hopeless situations. No situation is hopeless before your mighty power! I praise you, Father, for delivering me from fear, because you are a God of wonderful miracles and faithfulness to your people! Glory!

July 26 *"Fear not, for I am with you. Do not be dismayed. I am your God. I will strengthen you; I will help you; I will uphold you with my victorious right hand. See, all your angry enemies lie confused and shattered. Anyone opposing you will die. You will look for them in vain – they will all be gone. I am holding you by your right hand – I, the Lord, your God – and I say to you, Don't be afraid; I am here to help you. Despised though you are, fear not, O Israel; for I will help you. I am the Lord, your Redeemer; I am the Holy One of Israel." Isaiah 41:10-14 TLB*

I am thankful, Father, that you bring your people to victory no matter what the situation is. Your right hand is more powerful than all the armies of the world with all their weapons, and no one can stand against me because you are FOR ME! Thank you, Father, that I am victorious in ALL SITUATIONS!

July 27 *"But now the Lord who created you, O Israel, says, 'Don't be afraid, for I have ransomed you; I have called you by name; you are mine. When you go through deep waters and great trouble, I will be with you. When you go through rivers of difficulty, you will not drown! When you walk through the fire of oppression, you will not be burned up – the flames will not consume you.'" Isaiah 43:1-2 TLB*

How I praise you, Father, for redeeming me, for calling me by name, for rescuing me from trouble and difficulty and oppression, for saving me! Glorious Father, I rejoice that you openly declare in your Word that I am yours! Wherever I was, east, west, north or south, you called me to yourself because you love me, although my eyes were blind and my ears were deaf to your call. Because you are with me, I don't fear deep water, fire or all the power of the devil, for you will rescue me from all of them! Father, I praise you and thank you for who you are!

July 28 *"Don't be afraid of those who can kill only your bodies – but can't touch your souls! Fear only God who can destroy both soul and body in hell. Not one sparrow (What do they cost? Two for a penny?) can fall to the ground without your Father knowing it. And the very hairs of your head are all numbered. So don't worry! You are more valuable to him than many sparrows." Matthew 10:28-31 TLB*

How exciting, Father, to know that you love me so much you have even numbered the hairs on my head! Not only do you know those I have, you know those I have lost! I don't fear any person on this earth, because you notice the fall of the least sparrow to the ground, so you always know when I need your help and instantly you are right there with me. I praise you, Father, for getting rid of all my worries because you love me so much! I'm certainly glad I'm worth more to you than a sparrow!

July 29   *"The eternal God is your refuge, and underneath are the everlasting arms; He will thrust out the enemy from before you, and will say, 'Destroy!'" Deut. 33:27*

Father, I give praise to you for being the eternal God who has complete power over all things past, present and future. I thank you for forgiving all my sins of the past, for loving me right now and for giving me a wonderful future to look forward to! I praise you for holding me with love in your everlasting arms, because you are my refuge, and nothing can harm me regardless of the situation. Thank you for always going before me in your glory and power, so that the wicked are thrust out of my path. Father, I love your everlasting arms!

July 30   *"You shall also decide and decree a thing and it shall be established for you, and the light [of God's favor] shall shine upon your ways." Job 22:28 Amp.*

Bless you, Father, that I don't have to worry about whether or not I'm going to be a failure or a success, because your blueprint for my life makes it so simple. I'm throwing fear right out the window because you've said that when I decide and decree a thing it shall be established! How I praise you that I'm walking in the light of your favor and it's shining upon my ways! Glory, Father, what a privilege to be able to follow your Word so easily and know that you make us winners all the time. I love you for that!

July 31   *"Do not fret or have any anxiety about anything, but in every circumstance and in everything by prayer and petition [definite requests] with thanksgiving continue to make your wants known to God. And God's peace [be yours, that tranquil state of a soul assured of its salvation through Christ, and so fearing nothing from God and content with its earthly lot of whatever sort that is, that peace] which transcends all understanding, shall garrison and mount guard over your hearts and minds in Christ Jesus." Phil. 4:6,7 Amp.*

How I thank and praise you, Father, because I don't worry, fret or stew about anything, for your love for me is so great that I am filled with and surrounded by your mighty power at all times. Because of your promises and your Word, I have peace in all circumstances, the peace that surpasses all understanding, the peace that guards my heart and mind in Christ Jesus. I praise you for the wonderful blessing of that peace! Hallelujah!

AUGUST
GENERAL

August is the time when some people begin to drag because of the long, hot, summer days, but how we praise God for His Word, *"But they that wait upon the Lord shall renew their strength; they shall mount up with wings as eagles; they shall run, and not be weary; and they shall walk, and not faint." Is. 40:31.*

Let's mount up with wings as eagles and soar higher this month than we ever have. Let's confess these scriptures four and five times every day!

This month we're confessing scriptures which we have put under a "General" category. Some of these are the "old" favorites that really tell us what God has for us, and many of us are familiar with them, but we need to memorize and confess them to make them stronger in our daily lives.

Why not select at least two scripture verses each month to memorize. Say them out loud or in your thoughts every day as often as they come to your mind.

Aug. 1   *"But He answered and said, 'It is written, "Man shall not live by bread alone, but by every word that proceeds from the mouth of God."'" Matthew 4:4*

Father, I thank you that I don't have to exist only on earthly foods, because I live in an eternal realm as well as a temporal world. Thank you that our most delicious meals and desserts are the words which come out of your mouth! Thank you, Father, that your Word is true, and that everything you have said will come to pass because you spoke it, and you are a God who cannot lie. Thank you that I don't have to depend just on meat and potatoes for strength, but I can depend

on you from whom our real strength comes! Thank
you for saying, "It is written," because the devil has
to run when I say those words to him!

Aug. 2   *"And they overcame him by the blood of the Lamb
and by the word of their testimony, and they did not
love their lives to the death." Revelation 12:11*

Thank you, Father, that the blood of the Lamb overcomes all things, and makes us overcomers! I praise
you, Father, because the blood of Jesus was shed for
each and every one of us, and that blood is more powerful than the devil because he even trembles when He
comes close to that blood line which surrounds us! The
very word of my testimony gives me power over all of
the enemy! Thank you, Father, that when I speak your
Word, it becomes my word, and is power!

Aug. 3   *"The Spirit of the Lord is upon Me, because He has
anointed Me to preach the gospel to the poor. He has
sent Me to heal the brokenhearted, to preach deliverance to the captives and recovery of sight to the blind,
to set at liberty those who are oppressed." Luke 4:18*

Father, how I bless you that because I'm a joint-heir
with Jesus, this promise is mine. Thank you for making
such a wonderful job description for me so that I don't
have to worry about what I am to do. I'm sharing the
Good News, loving the brokenhearted who feel that
nobody loves them, and I'm speaking your words of
deliverance to those who are captive and slaves to habits
of the flesh. I praise you that your anointing is here at
all times, whether I feel like it or not. Thank you for
giving me such an exciting job!

Aug. 4   *"Finally, brethren, whatever things are true, whatever
things are noble, whatever things are just, whatever
things are pure, whatever things are lovely, whatever
things are of good report, if there is any virtue and if
there is anything praiseworthy – meditate on these
things." Philippians 4:8*

Father, I praise you because I don't have to think on or worry about the evil things of the devil. I don't have to worry about the problems of the world and the crises that arise. Thank you that I don't have to be in a continual state of being disturbed and tormented, because I follow your instructions and think on the beautiful uplifting things that are true, honest, just, pure and lovely. Thank you, Father, for telling me exactly upon what I should keep my eyes and mind. I love you, Father!

Aug. 5 *"For the weapons of our warfare are not carnal but mighty in God for pulling down strongholds, casting down arguments and every high thing that exalts itself against the knowledge of God, bringing every thought into captivity to the obedience of Christ"* **II Corinthians 10:4,5**

Thank you, Father, that our weapons are not of this world, but are spiritual because they come from you. Thank you for not expecting us to use carnal weapons, but for giving us such mighty spiritual swords! I praise you that I can cast down my imagination and the vanities that the devil would like to put into my mind, because I bring all of my thoughts to the wonderful obedience of Christ, because of your mighty power! Thank you, Father, that you control us!

Aug. 6 *"Let no corrupt communication proceed out of your mouth, but what is good for necessary edification, that it may impart grace to the hearers."* **Eph. 4:29**

Father, how I praise you for instructing me in what should come out of my mouth. Thank you for telling me that I shouldn't mock, ridicule, deny truth, confuse, or speak corruption in any way, because words that do not edify and minister grace to the person I am talking to, do not glorify you, and that is against what your Word says. Thank you for warning me that when I complain or criticize that those are foul and polluting words and totally unwholesome and worthless talk. I praise you that my every word can be used to glorify you at all times!

Aug. 7 *"But those who wait on the Lord shall renew their strength; they shall mount up with wings like eagles, they shall run and not be weary, they shall walk and not faint." Isaiah 40:31*

Today I feel like flying! I rejoice and thank you, Father, for the supernatural power and energy you give me. How I love you for telling me that when I serve and wait upon you that I can mount up like an eagle and draw close to you as the eagles draw close to the sun. Thank you that when I run I'm not weary, and when I walk I don't faint. Even when I'm tired, you give me that extra boost of energy, strength and vigor I need. When my enthusiasm begins to lag, and my zeal begins to sag, you're right there with those heavenly vitamins. I'm running with no weariness and walking joyfully and erect!

Aug. 8 *"Come to Me, all you who labor and are heavy laden, and I will give you rest. Take My yoke upon you and learn from Me, for I am gentle and lowly in heart, and you will find rest for your souls." Matt. 11:28,29*

I'm so rested, Father, I'm almost snoring, that's how relaxed I am! Thank you, Father, for the privilege of knowing that when I am faced with trials and problems I can come to Jesus, and He will give me rest from all of them. Thank you, Father, that your burden is light, and when we take your yoke upon us we have eternal, joyful rest in you. I praise you, because you are always there to take my burdens from me. How I praise you that your wonderful yoke is wholesome and good, and not harsh, hard, sharp or pressing, but comfortable, gracious and pleasant! Bless you for that divine rest!

Aug. 9 *"Call to Me, and I will answer you, and show you great and mighty things, which you do not know." Jer. 33:3*

I want to see more and more! I love you, Father, for always answering me when I call! Thank you that you didn't say you would answer me occasionally. You said all I had to do was call and you would be right there with the answer. Thank you that you said, in answer to my call for help, that you would show me great and mighty things which I don't even know about! Thank you, Father, that you show me the supernatural and new things concerning you all the time! I praise you! I'm calling and will continue to call because I want to see your glory and your power more than I ever have before. I delight in and want you to show me things beyond my wildest dreams or visions.

Aug. 10 *"But truly, as I live, all the earth shall be filled with the glory of the Lord." Numbers 14:21*

Father, I want to see your glory! I want to bask in the magnificence of your Presence, and I can hardly wait to see the entire earth filled with your glory! The joy of the saints is full of glory, and I want to see the whole earth filled with your saints who are full of glory and joy. Great is the glory of the Lord. I thank you that you are a sun and shield, and that you give grace and glory! Father, you are a shield for me; my glory, and the lifter of my head! I bless you that even though darkness covers the earth, and gross darkness the people, your glory shall be seen on us!

Aug. 11 *"So the ransomed of the Lord shall return, and come to Zion with singing, with everlasting joy on their heads; they shall obtain joy and gladness, and sorrow and sighing shall flee away." Isaiah 51:11*

I'm redeemed by the blood of the Lamb! I thank you that I can sing, sing, sing all the time because your everlasting joy is pouring upon my head at all times. I thank you that this is not just a temporary joy, but an eternal and everlasting joy which will never fade away and disappear. How I praise you, Father, that

you don't give me sorrow and sadness, but instead
you give me joy, joy, JOY! I love you because sorrow and mourning are fleeing away from my life just
as you have promised. How I love you and praise
you for all those covenant promises which are mine!

Aug. 12 *"The steps of a good man are ordered by the Lord,*
and He delights in his way." Psalm 37:23

Father, I rejoice that I'm walking in the steps you have
ordered. Thank you that you direct each and every step
I take. Thank you that I don't have to worry about the
direction I'm going, because you've ordered me to take
those steps, Father, and I'm walking exactly where you
tell me to walk. I rejoice because the way you direct my
steps is sure and true, superior to anything I could do to
find my own way. I'm delighted because it doesn't make
any difference if I'm going east, west, north or south,
you keep my footsteps going in the "right" direction. I
praise you because you aren't only interested in my entire trip, but you're interested in every single step I take!

Aug. 13 *"Do not neglect the gift that is in you, which was*
given to you by prophecy with the laying on of the
hands of the presbytery. Meditate on these things;
give yourself entirely to them, that your progress may
be evident to all." I Timothy 4:14,15

Father, I praise you that the Holy Spirit gave me that
special inward gift. I am practicing and cultivating and
meditating on all these things, so that your grace may be
evident to all. I am not going to neglect the helps you
have given me to live the Christian life or to minister in
the life of someone else, but I am stirring them up.

Aug. 14 *"God is my strength and power, and He makes my*
way perfect." II Samuel 22:33

Father, how I praise you that YOU are my strength
and my power. Thank you that I don't have to be

satisfied with the things of this world, and my own strength, but I praise you that you have given me your very own strength and power, and because of this you make my ways perfect. Father, thank you for being willing to make my way perfect because I'd never be able to do it on my own. I bless you that the energy I have comes from the mighty energy that Jesus Christ puts in me, energizing and empowering me to do what He wants me to do. Thank you that you are my strong fortress and that, because you guide me, you set me free! Bless you, Father!

Aug. 15 *"He gives power to the weak, and to those who have no might He increases strength." Isaiah 40:29*

Father, I love you even during my weaknesses and faults, because I know better than to rely on my own abilities, so I put my whole trust in you! Thank you for the power that you give to me when I'm weak and faint. Father, I praise you for the fact that when I'm all worn out and undone, you cause me to not look to myself and my solutions, but you give me strength, causing it to multiply and abound. Thank you that in my darkest moments of despair, you continually charge and recharge my spiritual batteries with supernatural strength! I worship you for that, Father!

Aug. 16 *"Blessed be the Lord, who daily loads us with benefits, the God of our salvation! Selah" Psalm 68:19*

I praise you, Father, and love you and worship you for loading me down with benefits day after day. Thank you that your blessings are not a one-time thing, but that you daily load me down with all your wonderful benefits, promises and blessings. My life would be as dry and parched as a desert, but you are a river to me! I bless you, the God of my salvation! As I look over this day, Father, I bless you because you don't just give us a little sampling of benefits. I'm excited that you have an overabundance of everything, so you load me and continue to load me with your

blessings and benefits! I can hardly contain myself,
Lord God!

Aug. 17 *"You will keep him in perfect peace, whose mind is
stayed on You, because he trusts in You." Isaiah 26:3*

How I love and adore you, Father, because my heart,
my mind and my soul have perfect and constant peace.
And, Father, all this is mine because you simply said
if I kept my mind on you and trusted, this would be
mine. I thank you for that perfect peace you give,
which the world can't understand, just because I trust
in you. Father, I thank you because you give me the
guidelines for keeping my mind on you so that I lean
on you and confidently hope and trust in you. Thank
you that my mind doesn't have to go to the things of
the world, but can confidently stay on you!

Aug. 18 *"Let not your heart be troubled; you believe in God,
believe also in Me. In My Father's house are many
mansions: if it were not so, I would have told you. I
go to prepare a place for you. And if I go and prepare a place for you, I will come again and receive
you to Myself; that where I am, there you may be
also." John 14:1-3*

Thank you, Jesus, for giving me an untroubled heart.
Thank you for that mansion which you've prepared
for me. I get so excited when I think about my new
house up there with all the things that I've ever wanted
in an earthly house, and even more, because of your
superabundance for me! I get jubilant when I think
about your return because I can hardly wait to live
with you and God forever and forever. Thank you,
Jesus, for giving me such an exciting future!

Aug. 19 *"I will bring the blind by a way they did not know; I
will lead them in paths they have not known. I will
make darkness light before them, and crooked places
straight. These things I will do for them, and not forsake them." Isaiah 42:16*

Bless you, Father, that once I was blind but now I see. I praise you that even before you saved me, you directed my footsteps so that I would go down paths that I would not have otherwise known. I praise you that my steps are ordered by the Lord and that you turn the darkness inside out and make it light, and that you take the most crooked path imaginable, and straighten it out with one single Word. Father, I praise you for your total and complete protection at all times.

Aug. 20 *"This is the covenant that I will make with them after those days," says the Lord: "I will put My laws into their hearts, and in their minds I will write them," then He adds, "Their sins and their lawless deeds I will remember no more." Hebrews 10:16,17*

Father, how I praise you that the one offering of your perfect Lamb has completely cleansed me! I love you for putting your laws right into my heart, and writing them into my mind. I don't depend only on memorizing words from the law, because your Holy Spirit reminds me of them constantly. Father, I love you for forgiving and forgetting all my sins and iniquities. I praise you that I don't have to remember them either, because you have forgotten them!

Aug. 21 *"The righteous cry out, and the Lord hears, and delivers them out of all their troubles." Psalm 34:17*

Lord, I tasted you and saw that you are good. I'm blessed because I trust in you. I thank you that I can bless you at all times and praise you continually, because when I cry out for help you are there to deliver me at all times. I magnify the Lord and I exalt your Holy name, because you always hear me. You have no hearing problems and your ears are tuned to the righteous at all times. Even though many evils confront me, you deliver me out of all of them. I bless you because you redeem the life of your servants, and none of us who take refuge in you shall be condemned or held guilty! Thank you for being my deliverer!

Aug. 22   *"As for Me," says the Lord, "this is My covenant with them: My Spirit who is upon you, and My words which I have put in your mouth, shall not depart from your mouth, nor from the mouth of your descendants, nor from the mouth of your descendants' descendants," says the Lord, "from this time and forevermore." Isaiah 59:21*

Father, I thank you for the covenant you gave to me. I thank you for the words which you have put in my mouth, because they are your words since you put them there. I praise you that your words shall not depart out of my mouth, nor out of the mouth of my children, nor out of the mouth of my grandchildren. Thank you, Father, for not only blessing me personally, but for blessing me down through the second and third generations. I praise you that their hearts will be so in tune with you that their mouths will be pure and speak your words at all times. I love you, Father, for this wonderful promise.

Aug. 23   *"Arise, shine; for your light has come! And the glory of the Lord is risen upon you." Isaiah 60:1*

Thank you, Father, that Jesus, the light of the world, lives in me and therefore your glory is also risen upon me. I praise you that I don't have to lie down and wallow in misery, but I arise from the depression and prostration in which circumstances have kept me, and constantly let your light shine through me. I thank you that I have risen to a new life and that I am radiant with the glory of the Lord. I get so excited when I know that your glory is risen upon me! I can't see it, but I praise you that the world can, just because you said so!

Aug. 24   *"These things I have spoken to you, that My joy may remain in you, and that your joy may be full." Jn. 15:11*

Father, how I praise you for your words, those words of hope, inspiration, assurance and security for all the problems of life. Those words have I hidden in my heart, that I might not sin against you, and when

I keep them safely tucked away in there to be a constant reminder to me of your love and perfection at all times, my joy remains, and my cup of joy is full and complete and overflowing. I thank you for this. My JOY is full! It isn't half full, it isn't a quarter full, it's full all the way up to the top because your Word says so!

Aug. 25   *"So, dear brothers, you have no obligations whatever to your old sinful nature to do what it begs you to do." Romans 8:12 TLB*

How I praise you, Father, that I have absolutely no obligation to my old nature! I don't ever have to do what it tells me to, and even when my old nature goes down on its knees and begs me to do something, I don't have to obey it because there are absolutely no obligations left to it. I bless you that I am in no way a debtor to that old carnal nature of mine, so that I no longer have to live a life ruled by the standard set up by the dictates of the flesh. I praise you, Father, because the old way was death, but the new way is LIFE! Hallelujah!

Aug. 26   *"And since we are his children, we will share his treasures – for all God gives to his Son Jesus is now ours too. But if we are to share his glory, we must also share his suffering." Romans 8:17 TLB*

Father, I praise you because I AM your child. I praise you that I share your treasures and have everything that you gave to Jesus! Hallelujah! I never understand why you're so good to us, but I thank you and praise you anyway because of what you give us. Thank you, Father, that you love us as much as you love Jesus, because this is one of the greatest of all treasures - that abiding, everlasting, continuing, overwhelming, eternal love! Glory!

Aug. 27   *"...one God and Father of all, who is above all, and through all, and in you all." Ephesians 4:6*

Father, how I love you because I don't have to worry
about which God to serve. You are the only true God,
the Father of us all, and you are sovereign above and
over all, so I don't have to worry about whose God is
best. How I praise you that you're living in every
part of me, my eyes, my nose, my mouth, my ears,
my arms, my hands, my fingers, my legs, my feet,
and even my toes. I look at my feet, Father, and
wonder how and why you would want to live in them,
but I love you because you live in every part of me!

Aug. 28   *"In you, O Lord, I put my trust; let me never be put to
shame." Psalm 71:1*

Praise you, Father, that my trust is in you; thank you
that I don't ever have to put my trust in confusion,
because there is too much confusion in the world already. I praise you that when problems arise and pres-
sure comes, I can stop being perplexed and confounded
and know that my trust is in you, in whom there is all
wisdom and truth. I thank you, Father, that I don't
have to search around and try to find someone whom
I can trust, but I am secure in the knowledge that I
can confidently take refuge in you at all times!

Aug. 29   *"In everything you do, stay away from complaining
and arguing, so that no one can speak a word of
blame against you. You are to live clean, innocent
lives as children of God in a dark world full of people
who are crooked and stubborn. Shine out among them
like beacon lights, holding out to them the Word of
Life." Phil. 2:14-16 TLB*

Thank you, Father, that we don't have to argue and
complain because you've given us a power that keeps
us above all of the things of the flesh. Thank you for
your instructions on how I can live a clean and innocent life. Father, I thank you that we are lights shining and beaming your love all over the world as we
hold out to all people your Word of Life. I praise you
for using me.

Aug. 30 *"He did not waver at the promise of God through unbelief, but was strengthened in faith, giving glory to God, and being fully convinced that what He had promised He was also able to perform." Rom. 4:20,21*

Father, I praise you that I don't have to stagger with unbelief or doubt at some of your promises, because what you promise you are exceedingly and abundantly able to fulfill. I praise you that your Word is full of promises for us and yet you are able to accomplish each and every one of them. I love you, Father, for being a God with whom all things are possible.

Aug. 31 *"...knowing this, that our old man was crucified with Him, that the body of sin might be done away with, that we should no longer be slaves of sin. For he who has died has been freed from sin." Romans 6:6,7*

Father, I praise you that I can go to my own spiritual funeral and see myself dead to sin! I praise you that in our dying to self you have totally and completely removed us from sin. I praise you for that end of self. I love you, Father, for giving me another month of victory and joy, and as this month goes by and becomes history, never to be relived again, I praise you that I don't ever have to live in the flesh again! Glory!

HEALING

HEALING IS FOR YOU!

One of the most beautiful things about salvation is that it not only includes the forgiveness of our sins, but the healing of our bodies as well. If we all understood the benefits of salvation, there would be healing for all the minute we are truly saved. However, if we don't get healed at that moment, healing is still for us because God wants you well. God does not want us sick!

When the devil attacks us and puts sickness on us, we know that we can call upon the name of Jesus for healing because there is tremendous healing in that name. The name of Jesus is above every disease. It's above cancer. It's above arthritis. It's above heart problems. It's above every disease that exists! We simply need to believe in the power in that name if we want to receive healing for ourselves.

God has also given us another avenue for healing because in Mark 16:18 the Bible says, *"[Those who believe] will lay hands on the sick, and they will recover."* We can go to a Spirit-filled believer and have them lay hands on us and receive the healing that we need. Jesus also said in Matthew 28:18, *"All authority has been given to Me in heaven and on earth."* Then in Luke 10:19, Jesus said to the believer, *"Behold I give you the authority to trample on serpents and scorpions, and over all the power of the enemy, and nothing shall by any means hurt you."* The power was His and then He gave it to us. This is the reason we can speak with authority when we speak healing over a believer who has been tormented by the devil. Let's speak our healing into existence right now. We are asking God to anoint this page so when you lay hands on it you will receive healing!

Sep. 1   *"Bless the Lord, O my soul, and forget not all His benefits: who forgives all your iniquities, who heals all your diseases." Psalm 103,2,3*

Father, I praise you for being the God who loves us so much that you even remind us in your Word not to forget ALL your benefits! Father, don't ever let me forget a single one of them, because I rejoice with open arms to receive all the blessings you want me to have! I thank you that all my sins are gone, gone, gone, and that you have healed ALL my diseases. I'm walking in divine health and I praise you for that! Thank you for redeeming my life from the pit and corruption and for beautifying me with your loving-kindness and tender mercies!

Sep. 2   *"He sent His word and healed them, and delivered them from their destructions." Psalm 107:20*

Thank you, Father, for sending your Word to heal us. Thank you that there is no sickness in your kingdom, and we don't have to be in bondage to disease and illness. I love you, Father, because the prescription to heal every disease is written in your Word! Thank you that we're delivered from all of our destructions, and healed of all our physical problems. Thank you for sending your Word of healing and deliverance! Thank you that there has not failed one word of all your good promises – in the past, the present, or the future! I love you and worship you for that!

Sep. 3   *"...If you diligently heed the voice of the Lord your God and do what is right in His sight, give ear to His commandments and keep all His statutes, I will put none of the diseases on you which I have brought on the Egyptians. For I am the Lord who heals you." Ex. 15:26*

I'm listening carefully, Father, and I praise you for talking long enough for me to hear your voice and for keeping your Holy Spirit constantly after me so that I will do what is right. Thank you for my ears which hear, and thank you for the promise that you won't put any of the diseases you gave the Egyptians on me. Thank you, Lord, that you bring Good News and healing! I praise you for being a disease-free God!

Sep. 4 *"But He was wounded for our transgressions, he was bruised for our iniquities; the chastisement for our peace was upon Him, and by His stripes we are healed." Isaiah 53:5*

I thank you, Father, for your wonderful Word of prophecy through Isaiah that predicted the suffering of your Son years before it happened! Thank you for the wounds that covered our transgressions. How I love Jesus for taking the bruises for our iniquities and the chastisement of our peace! Jesus, we can never thank you enough for that, but we keep trying our best. Thank you, Jesus, that those stripes on your back were taken for my healing. I praise you, Father, that I am healed because of the miracle of miracles that took place 2,000 years ago.

Sep. 5 *"...that it might be fulfilled which was spoken by Isaiah the prophet, saying: 'He Himself took our infirmities and bore our sicknesses.'" Matthew 8:17*

How we bless you and praise you, Father, that Jesus took every one of our infirmities and he accepted all of this sickness upon himself. We praise you, Father, that He didn't leave some of them out, but that He just made one big clean sweep of all the sicknesses in the entire world and bore each and every one of them for us. Thank you, Father, that because Jesus did this, we don't have to have sickness because there's no point in both of us having it. I'm not accepting sickness in my body, because then Jesus' sacrifice would have been in vain!

Sep. 6 *"My son, give attention to my words; incline your ear to my sayings. Do not let them depart from your eyes; keep them in the midst of your heart; for they are life to those who find them, and health to all their flesh." Proverbs 4:20-22*

Father, I'm listening! I'm attending to your Word. I've got my ear turned to you and tuned into you.

I've got my eyes glued to your words, and I'm not going to let them get out of my sight. I'm feeding on your Word, so it becomes a vital part of me, right in the midst of my heart! I praise you for the life that you have given to me through your Word, and for the health which I'm enjoying every day. I bless you, Father!

Sep. 7   *"...who Himself bore our sins in His own body on the tree, that we, having died to sins, might live for righteousness–by whose stripes you were healed."I Pet. 2:24*

Thank you, Father, for the cross where Jesus died, where He took upon Himself all of our sins so that I don't have a sin left against me. I praise you that He took each and every one of them and bore them so that I can and do live in your righteousness. How I love you for giving us that health through those stripes He endured, so that we could say, "Healing is mine!" Father, I praise you! I will confess those words over and over again, "By His stripes I was healed!" "By His stripes I was healed!" "By His stripes I was healed!" Hallelujah!

Sep. 8   *"...I have heard your prayer, I have seen your tears; surely I will heal you." II Kings 20:5*

Heavenly Father, thank you for looking down at me and seeing my tears. I don't understand how you could see each and every single tear I've cried, because they've been so many, but I praise you that not a single one of them escaped you. I don't fully understand all of your promises, but how I praise you that you so simply told me you would heal me. I love you, Father! From the innermost recesses of my heart, I thank you that you have HEARD my prayers, as insignificant or as improperly worded as they might have been. Glory!

Sep. 9   *"And the Lord will take away from you all sickness, and will afflict you with none of the terrible diseases* *of Egypt which you have known, but will lay them on all those who hate you." Deuteronomy 7:15*

Father, I'm healed before I get sick! Hallelujah! I praise you, Father, for taking away from me all illness and disease, because you love and protect those who are faithful to you. I praise you that, instead, you lay diseases on those who hate me, because those who hate your servants fall under your judgment, and your judgment is righteous. Thank you, Father, that your Word promises that you will take away from me ALL SICKNESS, and not just some sicknesses. I rejoice in the wonderful health you have given me, heavenly Father!

Sep. 10   *"A merry heart does good, like medicine, but a broken spirit dries the bones." Proverbs 17:22*

Father, I'm laughing right now! Ha, ha, ha, ho, ho, ho, he, he, he, because you said that laughter does us good like a medicine. I thank you for that dose of heavenly medicine which cures ills. Father, I'm going to laugh all day long because a merry heart brings healing like a medicine. Thank you for letting us know that we should have a good sense of humor. Thank you that I don't have to have a depressed mind or a broken spirit which dries up my bones, because you have renewed me! Thank you, Father, that we can give our brothers and sisters in Christ a dose of medicine when they need it by cheering their hearts with laughter. Ha, ha, ha, ho, ho, he he, he!

Sep. 11   *"Large crowds followed Jesus as he came down the hillside. Look! A leper is approaching. He kneels before him, worshiping. 'Sir,' the leper pleads, 'if you want to, you can heal me.' Jesus touches the man. 'I want to,' he says. 'Be healed.' And instantly the leprosy disappears." Matthew 8:1-3 TLB*

"I want to!" "I want to!" "I want to!" What wonderful words of life those are! How I praise you, Father, that Jesus wants to heal us. I love you because it is in the very heart of Jesus to WANT us to have all the good things in life. I bless you because your Word tells us that Jesus has no desire for us to be sick, because He WANTS to heal us! I praise you, Father, because you are a God who wants us in perfect and divine health!

Sep. 12 *"Behold, I am the Lord, the God of all flesh. Is there anything too hard for Me?" Jeremiah 32:27*

Father, I love you and praise you because you are THE God of ALL flesh! I praise you that you never do things half way, you always go all the way! I love you for that, Father! I'm so glad that nothing is too hard for you! I praise you that when my own situations become so big they overwhelm me, I can give them to you and rest safe and secure in the knowledge that NOTHING is too hard for you. Father, I worship you because that which I think is an insurmountable mountain, is just a stack of children's blocks that can easily be knocked over by you. Hallelujah!

Sep. 13 *"If you do these things, God will shed his own glorious light upon you. He will heal you; your godliness will lead you forward, and goodness will be a shield before you, and the glory of the Lord will protect you from behind. Then, when you call, the Lord will answer. 'Yes, I am here,' he will quickly reply." Isaiah 58:8-9 TLB*

Thank you, Father, for that glorious light you shed upon me. I thank you for your promises of healing and restoration. I thank you that your godliness leads me forward and your goodness is just like a shield for me, bringing me peace and prosperity. Thank you, that you're always there when I call, and thank you that you so quickly reply, "I am here!" Glory, Father, I'm overcome with your promises! Thank you for removing every form of false and wicked speaking, and for guiding me continually!

Sep. 14 *"The fear of the Lord prolongs days, but the years of the wicked will be shortened." Proverbs 10:27*

Heavenly Father, I praise you that my life is long. Thank you that because I love you and stand in awe of your majesty and greatness, you lengthen my days. I praise you that only the wicked will have their days shortened, because your Word says, "The wages of sin is death." I rejoice that we have favor with you, that you bless our days with health and peace of mind, that you reward the lives of the righteous. Thank you for always blessing me with all the good things in life. I love you!

Sep. 15 *"There is one who speaks like the piercings of a sword, but the tongue of the wise promotes health." Proverbs 12:18*

I praise you, Father, for giving me a wise tongue. I bless you because you have taught me to speak divine health. I praise you that you've taught me not to let any corrupt communication come out of my mouth and not to acknowledge the sickness of the devil, but instead I can confidently say, "I'm catching a healing!" when the devil tries to give me a cold. Father, I praise you because my own tongue brings your health into my life! I bless you for this! I thank you that a wise tongue speaks your Word, which brings healing to my body. Thank you for harnessing my tongue to bring it under control!

Sep. 16 *"A wholesome tongue is a tree of life, but perverseness in it breaks the spirit." Proverbs 15:4*

Father, my tongue is wholesome! I praise you that you are the one who has made this possible. I thank you that my tongue is a tree of life which brings health and happiness. Bless you, Father, that because you control my tongue I don't break down my spirit with contrary words. Thank you that I've given up the griping that brings discouragement, because the words which you speak through my mouth are gentle and have healing power. I love you for this, Father.

Sep. 17   *"So you shall serve the Lord your God, and He will bless your bread and your water. And I will take sickness away from the midst of you. No one shall suffer miscarriage or be barren in your land; I will fulfill the number of your days." Exodus 23:25,26*

I praise you, Father, that my bread is blessed, and so is my water. I thank you that you have taken sickness away from me and my family. I thank you that women can stand on your Word and not have miscarriages. I praise you that you have promised that the wombs of your children will not be barren. Thank you for every married person who has been wanting a baby, who can now claim that promise because they are serving you! I praise you, Father, for making the barren woman the joyful mother of many children! Glory!

Sep. 18   *"He also taught me, and said to me: 'Let your heart retain my words; keep my commands, and live.'" Proverbs 4:4*

Father, I love you and praise you because your words are written in my heart. I'm keeping them there by memorizing and confessing them, and because I know what your Word says, I'm keeping your commandments. Thank you, Father, that your Word has told me if I do this I will have a long and happy life. I'm holding fast to every word you have said. I'm confessing all of your promises, and I'm hiding them in the deepest recesses of my heart! I'm hiding them there so that I won't sin against you, Father!

Sep. 19   *"He heals the brokenhearted and binds up their wounds." Psalm 147:3*

I thank you, Father, that even though my heart has been broken into many parts, you put it all back together again. Thank you that you didn't leave me to gather up the pieces, but you gathered them all up for me and put them together in a whole and complete heart. Thank you that I didn't have to go into a corner and lick my wounds like a dog, because your loving care bound them up for me! Thank you for curing all my pains and all my sorrows. Thank you for those divine bandages with that everlasting healing power in them that you wrapped around all of my wounds. Hallelujah, Father, I love you for that!

Sep. 20 *"And the prayer of faith will save the sick, and the Lord will raise him up. And if he has committed sins, he will be forgiven." James 5:15*

Heavenly Father, thank you that I can pray for myself and yet I can also have others pray for me because you simply said the "prayer of faith" would heal the sick, Father, I praise you that when I am too sick to pray for myself I can depend on my friends and brothers and sisters in Christ to pray the prayer of faith for me. Thank you that you raise me from my sick bed and that if there's any sin in my life, you forgive me. Father, I praise you for the most wonderful life in the world - the Christian life.

Sep. 21 *"I shall not die, but live, and declare the works of the Lord." Psalm 118:17*

I praise you, glorious Father, for your Word which you have given us to stand on. Thank you for such a promise as this that I can rely on and declare to the world that your works are truly magnificent and wonderful! Thank you that even though the doctors tell me I have an incurable disease and that there is nothing they can do, I can declare your Word and know that I shall not die, but, live, and declare the wonderful works you have done for me. Thank you, Father, for your positive promises, which give hope to the most weak in heart. Father, I boldly declare your works! Glory!

Sep. 22 *"But for you who fear my name, the Sun of Righteousness will rise with healing in his wings. And you* *will go free, leaping with joy like calves let out to pasture." Malachi 4:2 TLB*

Father, I bless and praise you because there's healing in the wings of the Sun of Righteousness. I praise you that there are blessings in His wings, and one of them is healing. Thank you for setting me free so I can leap with joy like a calf let out to pasture! Father, no worldly joy compares with the joy I have because of the healing in those wings. Glory! I will continually praise you and respect and have awe for your name because of your good promises to ALL of your children!

Sep. 23   *"'For I will restore health to you and heal you of your wounds,' says the Lord." Jeremiah 30:17*

I praise you, Father, for another of your positive promises that you will restore health to me. I praise you that you didn't say you would have to think about it, you simply said that you would restore health to me. Thank you that you heal me of all my wounds whether they are of the body, mind or spirit. I rejoice that I can worship you and serve you as a whole, healthy person. Father, thank you for the best promises in the whole world! Thank you for being the best promise-giver, and the best promise-keeper in the entire world. I love you for that!

Sep. 24   *"Be not wise in your own eyes; reverently fear and worship the Lord, and turn [entirely] away from evil. It shall be health to your nerves and sinews, and marrow and moistening to your bones." Prov. 3:7-8 Amp.*

Father, I thank you that I don't have to be smart in my own eyes. I worship you, I praise you, I love you, I adore you, and because of you I turn entirely and completely away from all sin and evil. Thank you, Father, that because you taught me this, I have health to my nerves and sinews, and life-giving blood in the marrow of my bones. Thank you that my bones aren't dry and brittle but are moist and pliable, so I can reach out and accept your gift of health! I love you, Father!

Sep. 25   *"Blessings on all who reverence and trust the Lord – on all who obey him! Their reward shall be prosperity and happiness. Your wife shall be contented in your home. And look at all those children! There they sit around the dinner table as vigorous and healthy as young olive trees. That is God's reward to those who reverence and trust him." Psalm 128:1-4 TLB*

Thank you, Father, that I have your blessings because I reverence, trust and obey you. How we praise you for healthy children! Because we love you, you reward us even on this earth by giving us children as strong and healthy as young olive trees. Thank you, Father, for including healthy children in your promised reward of prosperity and happiness to those who love and serve you, because we rejoice to tell our children that it's you, our Father in heaven, who blesses, protects and prospers us! Glory, Father!

Sep. 26   *"The eyes of those who see will not be dim, and the ears of those who hear will listen." Isaiah 32:3*

Father, I praise you that you have given me eyes that see and ears that hear, for your Word says I have them. Because my eyes are not dim in spiritual matters, I am not fooled by the devil's temptations. Because my ears are not deaf in spiritual things, I am not deceived by the devil's wicked lies, I see and hear correctly because you have blessed me with physical health and spiritual discernment, and I praise you for that, Father. You are a wonderful God, loving, merciful and powerful!

Sep. 27   *"No evil shall befall you, nor shall any plague come near your dwelling." Psalm 91:10*

Thank you, Father, for protecting me from all illness and disease, because your Word promises that you won't let any evil or plague overtake me. I thank you for protection from colds, flu, boils, infections and plagues of any kind. Father, you are my physician and you have the best hospitalization plan in the world, which is for us to stay healthy! I praise you that you can heal anything that befalls us, and I love you for keeping me healthy so I don't have to get healed! Thank you for divine health! Thank you for that divine protection from accidents, too, Father, because that type of thing falls under the heading of evil. Thank you for that blood barrier around me that protects me from wicked tongues as well! Thank you for protection of ALL kinds.

Sep. 28   *"And when I passed by you and saw you struggling in your own blood, I said to you in your blood, 'Live!' Yes, I said to you in your blood, 'Live!'" Ez. 16:6*

Father, thank you for protection from hemorrhaging during childbirth or any other time. I praise and thank you that when my blood flows from me during an attack from the devil, I can stand on the rock of your Word and know that you say, "Live!" to me. Thank you for loving us so much that you want us to be healthy, whole and protected throughout our bodies. I praise you, heavenly Father, that when we see a brother or sister in distress or trouble from bleeding, we can use your Word and command hemorrhaging to stop. I love you, Father!

Sep. 29   *"So shall they fear the name of the Lord from the west, and His glory from the rising of the sun; when the enemy comes in like a flood, the Spirit of the Lord will lift up a standard against him." Isaiah 59:19*

How we thank you, Father, for your constant protection of our health and well being. Thank you for letting us know that the enemy is going to try to attack us over and over and over, but when he does come in like a flood, and it seems as though we might be swept under by the undertow of his wickedness, your Spirit is always there to lift up a standard against him. We praise you for your protection, your constant care and your lovingkindness, from the rising of the sun to the going down of the same!

Sep. 30 *"O Lord my God, I cried out to You, and You have healed me." Psalm 30:2*

Father, how we praise you that when our health has sagged or even seems to be gone completely, we can cry out to you and you heal us! I love you, Father, because when we get wounded in the battle of health, no matter how deep or painful those wounds are, you have promised in your Word to heal us. I praise you, Father, because things that are impossible with men are possible with you! You are a God of love and truth and victory, and I rejoice in your miraculous healing power and glorify you for it! Thank you for another month of victorious health. I thank you and praise you because your promises that I've confessed this month are true! Glory, Father!

HOLY SPIRIT

October is the month of POWER! Jesus told His disciples to go and preach the gospel to every creature, then He immediately put up a stop sign and said, "Wait!" He told them to go in the upper room and wait for the Holy Spirit because He knew they were powerless without the Holy Spirit. They didn't want Him to go away but He said, *"It is to your advantage that I go away; for if I do not go away, the Helper will not come to you; but if I depart, I will send Him to you. And when He has come, He will convict the world of sin, and of righteousness, and of judgment. He will glorify Me..." John 16:7, 8, 14.*

The minute the disciples received the baptism with the Holy Spirit and began to speak with other tongues, they immediately began to preach Jesus and glorify Him. Once you have the baptism with the Holy Ghost, you will not talk about the church, your pastor, the Sunday School class or things of that nature. You will talk about Jesus. In the first sermon that was preached after they received the power of the Holy Ghost, Peter talked about the power that is in the Name of Jesus. Many people refer to Him as "Lord," "Christ," "the Son of God," which are all His titles. But His Name is JESUS! You will notice that once you have received the baptism with the Holy Ghost you will call Him by His exciting name instead of His title.

If you've never received the power of the Christian life, which is the baptism with the Holy Spirit, you WILL after confessing the Word this month on the Holy Spirit!

To us, the Holy Spirit has always been a "double" portion. We can all pray in our native language, but praying with the Spirit is that double portion we all want and need!

One of the biggest surprises came when we realized there was a difference between the "gift of tongues" and the "prayer" tongues. This really helped clear up some of the confusion. We had always put them into one category, that of "speaking in tongues," and NEVER realized any difference at all, nor did we associate this with the power of the Holy Spirit. No wonder we thought, "Do all speak in tongues?" applied to us negatively.

Praise God for His grace because we are beginning to be aware more and more of the complete misunderstanding that exists concerning the outward sign of having been baptized with the Holy Spirit. Many people who praise God in their own private language have never received the "gift" of tongues to the assembly, and many never will.

Compare the difference between the "prayer" tongue that is for all, and the gift of tongues to the assembly that is not for all. When the anointing falls upon a person with a message FROM God, it is a message from heaven to earth. This is a message from God to His people and in order for the congregation to understand it, it must be followed by an interpretation into the language they understand. The person who has the "gift" or "ability" of interpretation has another gift to be manifested in partnership with the tongues spoken out. He receives the interpretation from God and transmits it to the congregation in their local language.

Now think back on what the "prayer" tongue is. It is just the reverse of the "public" tongue. It does not need an interpretation, because it is a prayer of intercession by the Holy Spirit directly to God. He is all wisdom and all knowledge. He understands all languages, so does not need anyone to interpret for him. The prayer is to him, and him alone, and not to be shared with anyone on the earth. Remember this is the "earth to heaven" conversation. *(I Corinthians 14:2)* The other is a "heaven to earth" conversation, and there is a difference! *(I Cor. 12:10)*.

Oct. 1   *"But you shall receive power when the Holy Spirit*
            has come upon you; and you shall be witnesses to Me
            in Jerusalem, and in all Judea and Samaria, and to
            the end of the earth." Acts 1:8

            I HAVE POWER! Do you know how I know this,
            Father? Because your wonderful Word says so! I have

ability, efficiency and might because of your Holy Spirit! I thank you that the Holy Spirit not only filled me, but was completely diffused throughout my very own soul! How I praise you for completely immersing and submerging me in the power of your Holy Spirit! How I bless you for giving me the boldness of a lion to speak and share the Good News at all times! I'm talking to my neighbors. I'm talking to my fellow-employees. I'm talking to the people I do business with! Father, I'm so bold today I'm going to share your Word with everyone I meet! Glory!

Oct. 2 *"If you then, being evil, know how to give good gifts to your children, how much more will your heavenly Father give the Holy Spirit to those who ask Him!" Luke 11:13*

I thank you, Father, that you never give us anything evil. I love you and praise you because everything you give to me is good. I always want to give the best to my children, and I thank you, Father, that you want to give the best to me. I'm so glad that you love me more than I could ever love a member of my family, and that you give me better gifts than I could ever hope to give my loved ones. I thank you that I am loved by you and that you have given me the gift of your precious Holy Spirit. Thank you that I don't have to speculate and wonder if it's good or evil, but that I KNOW that I KNOW that I KNOW that it is good because it is from you! Glory!

Oct. 3 *"And suddenly there came a sound from heaven, as of a rushing mighty wind, and it filled the whole house where they were sitting. Then there appeared to them divided tongues, as of fire, and one sat upon each of them. And they were all filled with the Holy Spirit and began to speak with other tongues, as the Spirit gave them utterance." Acts 2:2-4*

Heavenly Father, I love you because the rushing sound that came on the day of Pentecost came right from heaven! I thank you that it fell upon ALL of those there and that they were ALL filled with the Holy Spirit and began to speak in tongues as the Spirit gave them utterance. I thank you, Father, because you haven't changed your plan and you don't restrict the Holy Spirit to just a few, but you give it unselfishly to ALL of us. Father, I praise you for loving me just as much as you loved the disciples, and for giving me the same beautiful gift of the Holy Spirit.

Oct. 4   *"I indeed baptize you with water unto repentance, but He who is coming after me is mightier than I, whose sandals I am not worthy to carry. He will baptize you with the Holy Spirit and fire." Matthew 3:11*

I'm on fire, Father, but don't call the Fire Department! I want to keep this fire burning! I praise you that your promises have come down through the ages so that I, too, could receive the same baptism that the disciples did on the day of Pentecost! I thank you that the fire of the Holy Spirit burns out the chaff in my life but is itself a fire that cannot be put out or burned out! I bless you and praise you because this indwelling power enables me to live above the sin of the world with a complete dislike and distaste for the things of the world!

Oct. 5   *"...Walk in the Spirit, and you shall not fulfill the lust of the flesh." Galatians 5:16*

I'm walking and leaping and praising God in the Spirit! Thank you, Father, for making your Word so simple for me to understand. I'm responsive to and controlled and guided by your Holy Spirit at all times, and I'm walking, talking, and living in the Holy Spirit at all times. You alone empower me to do this because you enable me to look at the lust of the flesh without gratifying those desires which are of my human nature and not of you. I don't have to listen to the devil when he talks to me, because I'm walking in the Spirit in power and glory and overcoming the devil all the way! How I praise and love you!

Oct. 6 *"Likewise the Spirit also helps in our weaknesses. For we do not know what we should pray for as we ought, but the Spirit Himself makes intercession for us with groanings which cannot be uttered. Now He who searches the hearts knows what the mind of the Spirit is, because He makes intercession for the saints according to the will of God." Romans 8:26,27*

Glory, Father, I'm praying according to your perfect will! How do I know I am? Because your Word says so! How I bless you that you have given me such a beautiful prayer language with which to pray, because sometimes the problems of the world are so great upon my shoulders I don't know which way to turn, and I don't know what words to say, so I just pray in the spirit, and He intercedes and makes intercession for me. How I bless you that in the natural I might pray outside of your will, but in the Spirit I always pray in perfect harmony with your perfect will. How I praise you, Father, that the Holy Spirit rushes to my aid at all times!

Oct. 7 *"Therefore do not be unwise, but understand what the will of the Lord is. And do not be drunk with wine, in which is dissipation; but be filled with the Spirit." Eph. 5:17,18*

Father, I'm filled up all the way to the top and running over with your Spirit! I praise you for letting me be wise in your ways so I will know what your will is. Thank you for that personal advice about not being drunk with wine. I think of the times before I was saved when I was drunk on the wine of the world, but I praise you because my spirit can soar higher and be stimulated more with the new wine of the Spirit than it ever did on artificial means. Father, I love you for giving me power to know your will!

Oct. 8 *"But the Helper, the Holy Spirit, whom the Father will send in My name, He will teach you all things, and bring to your remembrance all things that I said to you." John 14:26*

Father, how I praise you that the Holy Spirit is my teacher! Thank you that the Holy Spirit is the Comforter, the Counselor, the Helper, the Intercessor, the Advocate, the Strengthener, and the Standby in all situations. I thank you that the Holy Spirit was sent to magnify Jesus. I thank you for not limiting the Holy Spirit to teaching me certain truths, but for sending him to teach me all things, and to bring ALL of what your Word says to my remembrance. Thank you, Father, that I can trust what the Holy Spirit brings to my mind, because it is ALL good, and ALL from you. Thank you for being so good to me!

Oct. 9   *"...But whoever drinks of the water that I shall give him will never thirst. But the water that I shall give him will become in him a fountain of water springing up into everlasting life." John 4:14*

I'm drinking at the springs of living water and I'm happy! I praise you, Father, for the living water. I love you for giving the living water to me because I never get parched and thirsty as long as I drink from that water. I thank you and praise you that it is a well within my very own soul that springs up into everlasting life. Father, I praise you that you took me out of all the dry years I spent with the devil, and that you put me where I shall never thirst again. Thank you for that well of water which is constantly welling up, flowing and bubbling continually within me unto eternal life.

Oct. 10   *"And I will pray the Father, and He will give you another Helper, that He may abide with you forever." John 14:16*

Father, I love you, love you, love you, that you have given me another Comforter, but even more than that, Father, I praise you because you have promised that He will abide with me forever and forever and forever. I praise you and thank you that the Holy Spirit is abiding in me right now, comforting me and accompanying me wherever I go. I praise you, Father, that the Holy Spirit is the Spirit of Truth which the world cannot take into its heart, because they don't recognize Him but you have given Him to me to live forever in my heart! I bless you, Father!

Oct. 11   *"But when the Helper comes, whom I shall send to you from the Father, the Spirit of truth who proceeds from the Father, He will testify of Me." John 15:26*

Thank you, Father, that the Holy Spirit testifies to me of Jesus. I praise you that the Holy Spirit is the Spirit of Truth who rightly divides that which is not true from that which is true. I praise you that I can always depend on the Holy Spirit to reveal the truth to me in all situations in the world, and also in your Word. I praise you, Father, that the Holy Spirit comes from you and not from the devil. I praise you, Jesus, that the Holy Spirit is constantly reminding me at all times of you and your love for me, of your sacrifice, and of your cleansing power. I thank you that He is also the Counselor, Helper, Advocate, Intercessor and Strengthener!

Oct. 12   *"And it shall come to pass afterward that I will pour out My Spirit on all flesh; your sons and your daughters shall prophesy, your old men shall dream dreams, your young men shall see visions." Joel 2:28*

Father, I'm going to stand right under the center of that spout! I praise you that you are pouring out your Spirit upon all flesh. I praise you that this includes me and I thank you for pouring it all over me. Thank you that you are giving some of us the ability to dream dreams and others to have visions and prophesy. I thank you and praise you, Father, because your Spirit is blessing me more than ever before. I praise you that you didn't restrict it to the Pentecostals, but that you have given it to the Baptists, the Methodists, the Catholics, the Presbyterians, the Episcopalians and to "whosoever" will!

Oct. 13   *"Therefore, brethren, we are debtors – not to the flesh, to live according to the flesh. For if you live according to the flesh you will die; but if by the Spirit you put to death the deeds of the body, you will live." Rom. 8:12,13*

I don't owe my flesh anything! Father, I thank you that I am not a debtor to the flesh, and therefore I don't have to live after the lust of the flesh, because you have plainly told me that if I do, I shall die. I thank you and praise you, Father, that through the power of the Spirit I am constantly putting to death the evil deeds prompted by the flesh, so that I may live! I thank you that it gets easier every day for me to turn from my carnal nature because through the power of the Holy Spirit constantly and habitually with me, I am putting to death the evil deeds prompted by my body.

Oct. 14   *"But the fruit of the Spirit is love, joy, peace, longsuffering, kindness, goodness, faithfulness, gentleness, self-control. Against such there is no law." Galatians 5:22,23*

I rejoice and praise you, Father, for the love in my heart. Thank you that the fruit of the Spirit, or the work which His presence within me accomplishes, includes giving me the kind of love I never had before. Thank you that I can now love the unlovely! I thank you that I am running over with joy and peace and longsuffering. I praise you for gentleness, goodness and faith. I praise you for meekness and self-control. I love you for giving me not just one of the fruits of the Spirit, but ALL of them! Thank you that I am a big bowl of spiritual fruit salad!

Oct. 15   *"For as many as are led by the Spirit of God, these are sons of God. For you did not receive the spirit of bondage again to fear, but you received the Spirit of adoption by whom we cry out, 'Abba, Father.'" Rom. 8:14,15*

I am a son of God! Father, I love you for leading me by your Spirit and for making me your child! I praise you for your Word which assures me that I won't be left out, because you say AS MANY AS ARE LED, and not just a selected few, are the children of God. Thank you that I'm not caught up in slavery to fear, Father, but instead I've been adopted into your very own family! I rejoice and thank you for the presence and power of your Holy Spirit, which enables me to do the greater things your Word promises!

Oct. 16 *"But this precious treasure – this light and power that now shine within us – is held in a perishable container, that is, in our weak bodies. Everyone can see that the glorious power within must be from God and is not our own." II Corinthians 4:7 TLB*

I praise and thank you, Father, for the light inside my physical body that is right this minute shining out of me upon the world. I thank you for a divine Light of the Gospel that shines so brightly that everyone knows it couldn't be from my own power but can only be YOUR power shining and glowing through me. I praise you Father, for making me a million-watt floodlight that shows the lost ones how to find you! I rejoice because the whole world can see that the grandeur and exceeding greatness of power and glory are yours!

Oct. 17 *"...Christ is not weak in his dealings with you, but is a mighty power within you. His weak, human body died on the cross, but now he lives by the mighty power of God. We, too, are weak in our bodies, as he was, but now we live and are strong, as he is, and have all of God's Power to use in dealing with you." II Cor. 13:3,4 TLB*

All of God's power is mine! Heavenly Father, how I praise you and worship you that Jesus is a mighty power within me. I thank you that His human body, though weak, died on a cross, but He was resurrected, and that He now lives by the mighty power of your Spirit. I thank you that even though we are weak in our bodies, we have all of your power to use to make our lives victorious at all times! Thank you, Father, for this divine privilege.

Oct. 18   *"Yet to us God has unveiled and revealed them by and through His Spirit, for the (Holy) Spirit searches diligently, exploring and examining everything, even sounding the profound and bottomless things of God – the divine counsels and things hidden and beyond man's scrutiny." I Corinthians 2:10 Amp.*

Father, I thank you that you have revealed the secrets of the universe to us by and through your Holy Spirit. I praise you that the Spirit searches everything completely, thoroughly, effectually, wholly and in every respect, and because I love you and obey you, You have made all of the things which are beyond man's scrutiny and investigation available to me! I praise you, Father, that because I have the mind of Christ, these truths are available to me!

Oct. 19   *"But the natural man does not receive the things of the spirit of God, for they are foolishness to him; nor can he know them, because they are spiritually discerned. But he who is spiritual judges all things, yet he himself is rightly judged by no one." I Cor. 2:14,15*

I rejoice because I am not a natural (or unspiritual) man, Father! Because I'm not natural, I can receive ALL of the wonderful things from the Spirit which would be nothing but foolishness and trivia to the natural man. He cannot accept or welcome the wonderful gifts and teachings of the Holy Spirit because He is totally incapable of accepting them, but you let me investigate and appraise all things because I,m a spiritual man because your Word says so! I praise you, Father, that even though I judge all things and all situations, I am judged of no man!

Oct. 20   *"What is the result then? I will pray with the spirit, and I will also pray with the understanding. I will* *sing with the spirit, and I will also sing with the understanding." I Corinthians 14:15*

I praise you, Father, that you give us two "hot lines to heaven." I thank you that I can pray and praise you with my mind and understanding, and I can also pray and praise you with my spirit through the power of the Holy Spirit! Sometimes there are feelings in my heart that just can't be expressed with the understanding because they are so overwhelming, and I thank you, Father, for giving me a special way to pray or praise you with my spirit to express those wonderful feelings! I thank you that I don't have to confine my singing to my understanding, but that my spirit can sing also!

Oct. 21 *"For he who speaks in a tongue does not speak to men but to God, for no one understands him; however, in the spirit he speaks mysteries." I Cor. 14:2*

Thank you, Father, that you have given me an unknown tongue with which to praise you. I praise you that this special language is a private, personal, distinctive and unique communication that I have with you. Men can't understand it, but you can, Father. I praise you that in the spirit I can utter secret truths to you and hidden things which I don't understand, but your Spirit understands my spirit and answers! Thank you, Father, for the mysteries which my spirit converses with you about, which I have no way of understanding or knowing about, so that you can answer my prayers even before I utter them with my own understanding.

Oct. 22 *"And the spirits of the prophets are subject to the prophets." I Corinthians 14:32*

Father, I praise you that you give us control over our own spirit. I thank you that when I speak in tongues I can stop and start at will, because the Holy Spirit is a gentleman and never forces me to do anything I don't want to do. I thank you, Father, that you have stored

in my human body the power of the Holy Spirit, so
that I can pray in tongues any time I want to, and I
can stop praying in tongues any time I want to. I love
you for this, Father. Thank you for the glorious privilege of singing in tongues whenever I want to, and
stopping whenever I want to!

Oct. 23   *"Now he who keeps His commandments abides in Him,
and He in him. And by this we know that He abides in
us, by the Spirit whom He has given us." I John 3:24*

I thank you and praise you, glorious Father, for we
know that you abide in us because of the Spirit which
you have given to us. Thank you, Father, that I don't
have to wonder and question whether or not I belong to
you because your very own Spirit within me testifies to
me that you dwell in me and you have given me this
positive proof that I am your child. I bless you, Father,
for telling us that you dwell, reside, live, stay and abide
in us which means you accept and endure us. Glory to
you, Father, for such a great promise.

Oct. 24   *"And the Spirit and the bride say, 'Come!' And let
him who hears say, 'Come!' And let him who thirsts
come. And whoever desires, let him take the water of
life freely." Revelation 22:17*

Father, I thank you and praise you that you said whosoever will may come and take of the water of life
freely. Thank you that I'm drinking at the fountain of
living water. Thank you that your Spirit called me
and thank you that you're not stingy with the flow of
that fountain, but you said that I can just drink and
drink and drink! Father, I am a glutton for that living
water, and I love you for giving from a bountiful
supply! My heart is overflowing with gratitude and
joy because of the wonderful things you say in your
Word. I praise you that my soul is constantly re-
freshed, supported and strengthened by it!

Oct. 25   *"Now when they bring you to the synagogues and
magistrates and authorities, do not worry about how*

or what you should answer, or what you should say. For the Holy Spirit will teach you in that very hour what you ought to say." Luke 12:11,12

How I praise and thank you, Father, that when I run into situations where I find it difficult to speak what is on my heart, and I don't know the answers, your Holy Spirit teaches me quickly and wisely exactly what I need to say! I thank you that I don't have to be anxious or worried, but that I can always depend on your beautiful Holy Spirit to teach me the right words to say under all conditions.

Oct. 26   *"No temptation has overtaken you except such as is common to man; but God is faithful, who will not allow you to be tempted beyond what you are able, but with the temptation will also make the way of escape, that you may be able to bear it." I Cor. 10:13*

Father, how I bless you for your Word. I'm so blessed because no enticement to sin, no matter where it comes from or where it leads to, will overcome me beyond human resistance because of your compassionate nature and understanding. I praise you because I can trust you to always provide the way out, so that I can be capable and strong and powerful to patiently bear up under whatever temptation comes my way. Father, because of your faithfulness to me, I shall be faithful to you, depending on your Word to keep me from falling on the slippery paths and ditches that lie alongside the straight and narrow path.

Oct. 27   *"And my speech and my preaching were not with persuasive words of human wisdom, but in demonstration of the Spirit and of power, that your faith should not be in the wisdom of men but in the power of God." I Corinthians 2:4,5*

Dear Father, I praise you that we don't have to be gifted orators with words that the world can't understand, but we simply have to be ordinary people who use your boldness to go out and share the gospel which you back up with the power of your Holy Spirit. I thank you that I don't have to worry about what I say, or to whom I say it, because your power will cause people to have faith in you and not in me. I love you, Father, for using me even though I'm nothing special except in your kingdom. Glory!

Oct. 28   *"...When the enemy comes in like a flood, the Spirit of the Lord will lift up a standard against him." Is. 59:19*

Father, how I praise you that when the enemy roars around like a lion, or comes pouring into my life like a flood, I don't have to worry one tiny little bit because your Spirit raises up a standard against him that puts him to flight! Father, I love you beyond measure because I don't have to be afraid of the devil! I know at all times that your Spirit in lifting up that standard drives off the enemy. Thank you, Lord, that I'm always on the winning side! Thank you that I don't have to worry whether it's a trickle or a flood, your Spirit is always there to raise the right-sized standard! Thank you that I have victory!

Oct. 29   *"...Not by might nor by power, but by My Spirit, says the Lord of hosts." Zechariah 4:6*

Heavenly Father, I praise you that I don't have to be a superman full of strength, nor a powerful individual who can shake mountains, because my battles are all won in the Spirit. I thank you, Father, that the same promise that you gave to Zerubbabel applies to me, that all things are accomplished not by might, nor by power, but by your Spirit. I rejoice, Father, because your Spirit dwells in me! I thank you, Father, that the oil of the Holy Spirit is a never-ending source of oil, and not controlled by the countries or nations of the world, but by you. Hallelujah!

Oct. 30   *"It is the Spirit who gives life; the flesh profits nothing. The words that I speak to you are spirit, and they are life." John 6:63*

How I praise you, Father, that it is the Holy Spirit who quickens my mind to understand the truths of your Word and the truth of statements made to me. I thank you, Father, that your words are spirit and life. I thank you that because of your Holy Spirit, your Word is alive and living in me today! I thank you that I don't have to be dead in sin the way I was, but that I now have life in the Spirit! I know that my flesh conveys no benefit whatever, and there is no heavenly profit in it, but it is your life-giving Spirit that has made me come alive in Christ. I worship and praise you for that, Father!

Oct. 31 *"And these signs will follow those who believe; In My name they will cast out demons; they will speak with new tongues; they will take up serpents; and if they drink anything deadly, it will by no means hurt them; they will lay hands on the sick, and they will recover." Mark 16:17,18*

I'm a believer! Father, how I praise you because you have promised that through your Holy Spirit, signs follow me because I believe! I thank you that I can use the name of Jesus and cast out devils and speak with new tongues! I thank you that serpents can't harm me, and if I accidently drink something poisonous, your Spirit will protect me! I thank you, and praise you, Father, that because of the power of your Holy Spirit, sick people recover when I lay hands on them! Hallelujah! Thank you for the signs that follow me wherever I go!

November
Praise
And
Thanksgiving

November is the month of Thanksgiving and "thanks" giving! It's a time of great joy to all of us as we settle back and remember ALL the things we need to thank God for on the special day that we set aside to praise God for our bountiful way of life!

We thank God for Jesus, the rock of our salvation. *"The Lord is my rock, my fortress and my deliverer"* **II Samuel 22:2**

We thank God for salvation through the blood of Jesus Christ. *"In Him we have redemption through His blood..."* **Eph. 1:7**

We thank God for our marriage. *"Therefore what God has joined together, let not man separate."* **Matthew 19:6**

We thank God for our children. *"Like arrows in the hand of a warrior, so are the children of one's youth."* **Psalm 127:4**

"And my God shall supply all your need according to His riches in glory by Christ Jesus!" **Philippians 4:19**

We thank God for our grandchildren. *"Children's children are the crown of old men..."* **Proverbs 17:6**

We thank God for our ministry. *"And He Himself gave some to be apostles, some prophets, some evangelists, and some pastors and teachers, for the equipping of the saints for the work of ministry, for the edifying of the body of Christ."* **Ephesians 4:11,12**

We thank God for His Word. *"Heaven and earth will pass away, but My words will by no means pass away."* **Mark 13:31**

We thank God for faith..."*God has dealt to each one a measure of faith."* **Romans 12:3**

Let's confess these praise and thanksgiving confessions at least ten times each day so that our spirits will be soaring in the heavens every day this month.

Nov. 1   *"I will bless the Lord at all times; His praise shall continually be in my mouth." Psalm 34:1*

Father, we bless you, we bless you, we bless you! All day long I bless you because of your goodness to me. I bless you because you are the magnificent Creator who put the stars in the sky and separated the land from the sea. I bless you because you always keep your promises to us, even when fulfilling them requires miracles! I bless you, Father, because you have lifted me out of darkness and led me to victory. I bless you and praise you, for your praises are sweeter than honeycomb in my mouth. I praise you for your faithfulness to me. I praise you, Father, because it blesses me to keep your praises continually on my lips!

Nov. 2   *"Be glad in the Lord and rejoice, you righteous; and shout for joy, all you upright in heart!" Psalm 32:11*

Glory, Father, I'm filled to overflowing with gladness in you! I'm glad because my whole life is in your hands. I can't stop rejoicing because you have made me righteous through your glorious righteousness! You have made me upright because your strength is a never-failing support! I can't keep silent because if I did the very rocks would cry out, but I don't want to keep silent, for my heart tells me to shout for joy! Father, I have to sing and shout for joy because you've not only given me a wonderful day today but you've given me a wonderful future to look forward to in this life and the next – you've given me a wonderful forever.

Nov. 3   *"Let my mouth be filled with Your praise and with Your glory all the day." Psalm 71:8*

My mouth declares your praises, Father, because in all ways you are worthy of our praise! I honor and rejoice in your name! Father, I really want to thank you that my mouth doesn't have to be filled with mockery and scorn, with contempt and complaints, with deceit and accusation - the filth of the world - because I'm so filled with joy in praising you and your goodness that the world's conversation habits don't interest me in the slightest. I praise and honor you because in all the blessings you bring to me and to my family – love, joy, peace, health and prosperity – the glory belongs to you, Father. I honor you because you are a righteous and loving God, the fountainhead of all blessings.

Nov. 4 *"It is good to give thanks to the Lord, and to sing praises to Your name, O Most High." Psalm 92:1*

Heavenly Father, I rejoice and give thanks to you because you fill my life with so many good things that I overflow with feelings of thankfulness. I praise you, Father, and I thoroughly enjoy the abundance of blessings you bring to me because of who you are! How can I not be thankful for each bite of food when I love the Provider with all my heart? It is good to give thanks to you and sing your praises because it pleases you and because it lifts up our hearts to you. By thanking you, I send you my love. By singing your praises, I send you my love. Thank you for the joy you put in my heart even from thanking you!

Nov. 5 *"Make a joyful shout to the Lord, all you lands! Serve the Lord with gladness; come before His presence with singing. Know that the Lord, He is God; it is He who has made us, and not we ourselves; we are His people and the sheep of His pasture. Enter into His gates with thanksgiving, and into His courts with praise. Be thankful to Him, and bless His name." Psalm 100:1-4*

Father, I'm making a joyful noise because I only want to talk about you and to celebrate your Presence in my life with praise and thanksgiving. I serve you gladly with all my heart and mind, body and soul, and I can't stand in your Presence without singing because you have made me so glad to be your child! I praise you that we can enter your gates with thanksgiving and I thank you that we can enter your courts with praise. I bless and praise you, heavenly Father.

Nov. 6   *"I will praise You, O Lord my God, with all my heart, and I will glorify Your name forevermore." Ps. 86:12*

I praise you, Father, with all of my heart and all of my very being! I thank and praise you, because you made provision for forgiveness of my sins, you saved me from a life of eternal damnation through the sacrifice of your beloved Son, and you rescued me out of the miry clay to set my feet on solid rock. Glory, Father, I'm blessed to sing your praises because there is so much for which to praise you! I love you and praise you with every fiber of my being and I will glorify and lift up your holy name forever!

Nov. 7   *"I will sing to the Lord as long as I live; I will sing praise to my God while I have my being." Ps. 104:33*

Father, I thank you for the privilege of singing to you as long as I live. Singing to you is special to me, Father, because each song is an expression of thankfulness that reaches deep inside me to present an offering of joy beyond words. When I praise you in song, I feel as though you are touching me as I sing, as though you are lifting me up to you on the wings of that song. Heavenly Father, I thank you for listening to my songs because they always make me feel especially close to you. As long as there is breath left in my body, I will sing praises to you!

Nov. 8   *"Let the heavens rejoice, and let the earth be glad; and let them say among the nations, 'The Lord reigns.'" I Chronicles 16:31*

Glory, Father, the heavens are glad, the earth rejoices, and I'm saying over and over, THE LORD

REIGNS, THE LORD REIGNS, THE LORD REIGNS! Thank you, Father, for the way my spirit leaps within me when I say these wonderful words, THE LORD REIGNS! I praise you for even putting into my heart and mouth these words that make my soul sing: THE LORD REIGNS! You are the Creator and the Lord of all creation, and I rejoice with the earth and join in heaven's gladness, because you are my Lord and you rule over my life as well as everything else - visible and invisible! Father, I'm overwhelmed with thankfulness, because even though you have so much to care for, you take wonderful care of me!

Nov. 9   *"Therefore by Him let us continually offer the sacrifice of praise to God, that is, the fruit of our lips, giving thanks to His name." Hebrews 13:15*

Father, I offer the sacrifice of praise to you continually, even though it's no sacrifice to praise you, but a wonderful privilege. It gives me joy to praise you continually because you bless me continually. You even bless me by the lift you give me while I'm praising you! Father, the fruit of my lips is always good fruit in giving thanks to your name and praising you for just being who you are. Let the fruit of my lips send out the fruit of your Spirit: love, joy, peace, longsuffering, gentleness, goodness, faith, meekness and temperance. Father, you are the God of glory, and I love to praise you!

Nov. 10   *"Then I will praise God with my singing! My thanks will be his praise – that will please him more than sacrificing a bullock or an ox. The humble shall see their God at work for them. No wonder they will be so glad! All who seek for God shall live in joy. For Jehovah hears the cries of his needy ones, and does not look the other way. Praise him, all heaven and earth! Praise him, all the seas and everything in them!" Psalm 69:30-34 TLB*

I praise you, Father, while I'm singing. I thank you for all the good things in life. I praise you and thank you for my family, for my health, my life, and most important of all, for my salvation. Father, I join my voice with all the things in heaven and earth and praise you. My voice is not as loud or strong as the sea, but I praise you with all my might!

Nov. 11   *"Let everyone bless God and sing his praises, for he holds our lives in his hands. And he holds our feet to the path." Psalm 66:8,9 TLB*

Heavenly Father, we bless you and we sing, sing, sing your praises! Just as you hold all Creation in your hands, you hold our lives right in the hollow of your hands – and I bless and thank you for that, because in your hands we have everything – breath, life, and our very being. I bless you, Father, for saving, guiding, teaching and nourishing me. You've given me not just life, but all the trimmings with it, and it's a wonderful life because you constantly show me how you want me to live and what you want me to do. You light the path in front of me, you hold my feet on that path and you guard me from stumbling. Father, I bless you for this!

Nov. 12   *"From the rising of the sun to its going down the Lord's name is to be praised." Psalm 113:3*

It's early in the morning, Father, and I'm praising you before I even get out of bed. I praise you because I have a warm bed to sleep in and a roof over my head. I praise you because the sun rises each day on your beautiful creation and because the bright flowers, grass and lofty trees testify to your glory. I praise you for the sunshine, for the rain, for the seasons and for the food you put in my mouth. I praise you for all the wonderful things you give me to do each day and for opportunities to tell people about you. My lips are going to praise you this whole day long until the sun goes down, and then Lord, I'm going to keep praising your name. Hallelujah!

Nov. 13   *"...Believe in the Lord your God, and you shall be established; believe His prophets, and you shall prosper. And when he had consulted with the people, he appointed those who should sing to the Lord, and who should praise the beauty of holiness, as they went out before the army and were saying: 'Praise the Lord, for His mercy endures forever.' Now when they began to sing and to praise, the Lord set ambushes against the people of Ammon, Moab, and Mount Seir, who had come against Judah; and they were defeated."*
II Chronicles 20:20-22

Father, I praise you that I am established and am prospering. I praise you for the fantastic power that there is in praise. Thank you, Father, that when the enemies came after your children, the very moment they began to sing and praise, you caused the other armies to begin fighting among themselves, and they were destroyed! Thank you, Father, that because I am your child, I'm on the winning side at all times! Hallelujah!

Nov. 14   *"For I will pour water on him who is thirsty, and floods on the dry ground; I will pour My Spirit on your descendants, and My blessing on your offspring." Isaiah 44:3*

Pour it on me, Lord, because I'm thirsty! I praise you that you don't give me a tiny little straw to sip water when I'm thirsty, but you pour it all over me. I thank you that there is so much that it even pours off of me and floods the dry ground. Thank you that there is not only enough for me, but also for my offspring. I thank you that my children and their children are splashing in the overflow that you've given to me. I will bless you at all times, and your praise shall continually be in my mouth!

Nov. 15   *"And when the trumpeters and singers were in unison, making one sound to be heard in praising and* *thanking the Lord, and when they lifted up their voice with the trumpets and cymbals and other instruments for song, and praised the Lord, saying, 'For He is good, for His mercy and lovingkindness endure for ever,' then the house of the Lord was filled with a cloud, so that the priests could not stand to minister because of the cloud; for the glory of the Lord filled the house of God."* **II Chronicles 5:13,14 Amp.**

Your glory surrounds praise! I praise you because the minute we begin to praise and bless you, your glory fills the temple to such an extent that at times we can't even stand on our feet. Bless you, Father, that you don't reserve all the good things for heaven, but you even let us have some of your glory down here! Bless you for power and majesty and glory so strong that I can't even stand up!

Nov. 16   *"...your love and kindness are better to me than life itself. How I praise you! I will bless you as long as I live, lifting up my hands to you in prayer. At last I shall be fully satisfied; I will praise you with great joy."* **Psalm 63:3,4 TLB**

Father, I search for you and my soul thirsts for you, I rejoice in you, my God, because through the night you protect me in the shadow of your wings. My protection and success come from you alone. No enemy can reach me because of your love and kindness. Thank you for leading me to the mighty, towering rock of safety. I shall forever live in your tabernacle in the shelter of your wings. Thank you for all the blessings you reserve for those who call on your name!

Nov. 17   *"Oh, give thanks to the Lord! Call upon His name; make known His deeds among the peoples. Sing to Him, sing psalms to Him; talk of all His wondrous works. Glory in His holy name; let the hearts of those rejoice who seek the Lord. Seek the Lord and His strength; seek His face evermore. Remember His* *marvelous works which He has done, His wonders, and the judgments of His mouth." Psalm 105:1-5*

Father, I sing praises to you. I talk of all your deeds and devoutly and earnestly make them known. Father, my heart rejoices because I seek you as my indispensable necessity. I thank you that you are always there. Father, I shall seek your face all the days of my life and will remember all the wonderful and exciting deeds you have done. Hallelujah!

Nov. 18   *"Oh come, let us sing to the Lord! Let us shout joyfully to the Rock of our salvation. Let us come before His presence with thanksgiving; let us shout joyfully to Him with psalms. For the Lord is the great God, and the great King above all gods." Psalm 95:1-3*

We praise you, glorious Father, and sing songs before you and make a joyful noise to you because you are the Rock of our salvation, and our hearts just want to glorify you! I make joyful noises to you, Father, with thanksgiving in my heart and I enter before your presence with thanksgiving and songs of praise, because you do so much for me that I just want to rejoice and celebrate before you! Father, I praise and thank you because you are a great God, and a great King above all gods, and you are MY GOD!

Nov. 19   *"Teach me Your way, O Lord; I will walk in Your truth; unite my heart to fear Your name. I will praise You, O Lord my God, with all my heart, and I will glorify Your name forevermore. For great is Your mercy toward me, and You have delivered my soul from the depths of Sheol." Psalm 86:11-13*

Father, I praise you for teaching me your ways so I can avoid the deceptions of the devil, and walk in the truth. Tell me what to do and I will do it. Tell me where you want me to go and I will go there. Every fiber of my being unites in reverence and praise to your name. With every single bit of my heart I praise you and give glory to you because you are so kind to me and have rescued me from deepest hell! Father, how could I help but praise you constantly?

Nov. 20 *"But let the righteous be glad; let them rejoice before God; yes, let them rejoice exceedingly. Sing to God, sing praises to His name; extol Him who rides on the clouds, by His name YAH, and rejoice before Him." Psalm 68:3,4*

Heavenly Father, I am uncompromisingly righteous because of your power, and I'm glad of it. My spirit is high, and I jubilantly rejoice because I worship, follow and obey the God of glory and righteousness! Father, just praising you makes my entire spirit and soul feel merry. My mouth is filled with your praise and your honor all day long, for you are the Lord of creation, the great God over the heavens. I sing your praises because my tongue can't keep still in my mouth, I love you so much. Father, I rejoice before you - Jehovah is your name!

Nov. 21 *"Oh, clap your hands, all you peoples! Shout to God with the voice of triumph! For the Lord Most High is awesome; He is a great King over all the earth." Psalm 47:1,2*

Father, we clap, clap, clap our hands and rejoice with all our hearts and all our minds as we shout triumphant praises to you, for you are the Lord above all lords, the God above all gods, and you are awesome beyond words. The nations rise and fall at your command, and all the presidents, kings, premiers and other world leaders have their power only because you allow it. Kings and kingdoms come and go, but your reign is forever, heavenly Father. I praise you because your power is exercised in righteousness and love toward all your people. Father, I thank you and praise you and shout praises to you at the top of my lungs because of who you are! Glory!

Nov. 22 *"Oh, praise the Lord, for he has listened to my pleadings! He is my strength, my shield from every danger. I trusted in him, and he helped me. Joy rises in my heart until I burst out in songs of praise to him. The Lord protects his people and gives victory to his anointed king." Psalm 28:6-8 TLB*

I bless you, Father, because you hear me whenever I cry out to you for help. I praise you because you are my entire strength in time of need, my impenetrable shield in time of danger. You are with me always, and I fear no evil, not even the devil himself! My heart just relaxes, my tensions disappear, because I trust, rely on and confidently lean on you, and, Father, you never let me down. Because I am victorious in you, my heart is filled with joy, and I sing your praises!

Nov. 23 *"I will declare Your name to My brethren; in the midst of the congregation I will praise You." Psalm 22:22*

I'll gladly praise you and talk about you to my relatives, Father, and you'll be there to soften their hearts and open their ears, because I can't handle some of that stubbornness of theirs without your help. Still, I'll praise you - because when they come to know you as I know you, Father, they'll want to praise you too! I will even stand up in front of the congregation, Father, and tell about all the wonderful things you have done. I will publicly state all my vows to you in the presence of those who love you and worship you, and I'll praise you in the midst of them. My heart rejoices with everlasting joy, and I worship you.

Nov. 24 *"...then each one's praise will come from God." I Corinthians 4:5*

Glory, Father, I praise you that on the very special day when we stand before you in judgment, you will examine us even to the most secret places of our hearts, then the praise will be turned around and YOU WILL GIVE TO US PRAISE AND COMMENDATION for the things we have done on earth! Father, I always thought on that day I would have an opportunity to thank you in person for all the wonderful things you did for me down here on this earth! I thought I'd be able to thank you face to face for saving me, but your Word says you're going to thank ME! I don't know how that can be, Lord, but I rejoice at the thought of that wonderful day to come! I'm going to do more for you than ever before, so I'll have lots of time to spend listening to you on that great day! That really turns me on, Father!

Nov. 25 *"In God I have put my trust; I will not be afraid. What can man do to me? Vows made to You are binding upon me, O God; I will render praises to You." Psalm 56:11,12*

Father, I praise you and thank you because my trust is entirely in you and not in my own strength, for with you as my fortress I'm not going to fear what any man can do to me. Criticism and ridicule can't harm me, for I am shielded by your truth. Enemies can't touch me, for you confound and confuse them, and they are defeated by your strength. I rejoice that vows made to you are binding upon me, Father, because in your strength and power and faithfulness, my victory is assured in all circumstances! Because I trust you with all my heart, you've made me a winner, Father, and I sing your praises!

Nov. 26 *"Give unto the Lord, O you mighty ones, give unto the Lord glory and strength. Give unto the Lord the glory due to His name; worship the Lord in the beauty of holiness." Psalm 29:1,2*

Thank you, Father, that I can come before you with praise, giving you the glory and strength you deserve for all you have done and are doing for your people. I glorify you, Father, for passing on to me the inheritance of Abraham. I glorify you for giving us your Word, so that we can find instruction and understanding. I glorify you for my salvation and the blessings that go with it. You are a mighty God, O Father, and you deserve all glory! I rejoice to worship you in the beauty of holiness!

Nov. 27 *"Oh, sing out your praises to the God who lives in Jerusalem. Tell the world about his unforgettable deeds...He does not ignore the prayers of men in trouble when they call to him for help." Ps. 9:11-12 TLB*

I praise you, Father, and sing your praises around the world! My tongue just won't keep still, but breaks out in songs of praise, because you always hear us when we call to you, no matter what kind of trouble we are in. I praise you, Father, for your love and power, because your deeds in behalf of your people include many miracles, signs and wonders, and I will tell the world about them so that your name is glorified among all the people of the earth! And how I bless you for not ignoring my prayers when I'm in trouble and yelling for help!

Nov. 28 *"I will love You, O Lord, my strength. The Lord is my rock and my fortress and my deliverer; my God, my strength, in whom I will trust; my shield and the horn of my salvation, my stronghold. I will call upon the Lord, who is worthy to be praised; so shall I be saved from my enemies." Psalm 18:1-3*

How I love you, heavenly Father, because of all the tremendous things you have done for me. I praise you because you provide all that I need for my life. You are MY rock, for I stand on the truth of your Word. You are MY fortress, for I am safe in you. You are MY strength, for I am victorious in you. You are MY high tower, for I have wisdom in you. You are MY deliverer, MY salvation and MY God, for without you I would be lost in sin and darkness. I praise you Father, for lifting me into your marvelous light!

Nov. 29 *"Let them praise His name with the dance; let them sing praises to Him with the timbrel and harp." Psalm 149:3*

Father, I praise you with my dancing. I praise you for creating dancing as a form of worship to you, and just because the devil got into dancing doesn't mean I shouldn't worship you in the dance. I thank you for revealing the devil as a deceiver who wants to hurt and limit righteous worship any way he can. Sometimes, Father, I get so filled with rejoicing in you and your music, I just have to clap my hands and move my feet! I sing your praises while I dance, and I'd play a tambourine or a harp if I could, just to praise you even more and glorify your name!

Nov. 30 *"Praise Him with the timbrel and dance; praise Him with stringed instruments and flutes! Praise Him with loud cymbals; praise Him with high sounding cymbals! Let everything that has breath praise the Lord."*
Psalm 150:4-6

I praise you, glorious Father, with everything I have that makes noise because your Word tells me to make a joyful noise to you. Father, I clap my hands and sing and stamp my feet, just because I want to put everything I've got into worshipping and praising you! I can't play a timbrel or guitar or organ, but I can bang two of my kitchen pan lids together to sound like cymbals! Father, because I have breath in me, I praise you, praise you, praise you! As long as I have breath, I'll continue to praise you! Thank you for another wonderful month!

Sᴀʟᴠᴀᴛɪᴏɴ

As we wrote the confessions for December, they seemed to flow easier than any we've ever written.

...Maybe it was because we've written them for twelve solid months!

...Maybe it was because we felt a special anointing as we wrote them.

...Maybe it was because we have a special love in our hearts for you.

...Maybe it was because salvation is where it all starts. We pray as you confess them with us that your salvation will become more real and personal to you than it ever has been before. We know ourselves that as we wrote these confessions, we once again became powerfully aware of the sacrifice of Jesus in our behalf.

Dec. 1 *"But as many as received Him, to them He gave the right to become children of God, even to those who believe in His name." John 1:12*

I received Jesus, and you received me! Father, I praise you that because I accepted Jesus as my Savior and Lord, you gave me the right, privilege and power to become your child. Thank you that because I believe on His name I am restored to the fullness of your love which is much greater than even the love we have for our own children. I thank you and praise you that the gates of heaven have been opened to me because you sent your very own Son to call me to my eternal inheritance of everlasting life! I love you and worship you because you don't care what I used to be, you only see me for what I am today, YOUR CHILD! Hallelujah, Father, how I praise you for that wonderful blessing!

Dec. 2 *"...unless one is born again, he cannot see the kingdom of God." John 3:3*

Thank you, Father, for sending your Son to tell us the wonderful way you have given us to see the kingdom of heaven. I'm rejoicing because I've been born again of the Spirit and I praise you for making the truth so simple for me. Father, I love you because you didn't set up some difficult and complicated test I had to pass to get into your kingdom, you simply said I would have to be born again! I praise you that I don't have to guess or wonder about this because you have given me the answer to eternal life in that one little sentence spoken by Jesus. Thank you, Father, for opening the windows of heaven to me! Thank you that because I have been born again I can and will see your Kingdom!

Dec. 3 *"...I am the way, the truth, and the life. No one comes to the Father except through Me." John 14:6*

I praise you, Father, that your Word makes the way to salvation and eternal life so clear and uncompromisingly direct. Jesus quite plainly said there was no other way to come to you except by Him. I praise you, Father, that I'm not wasting time searching around for the way into heaven, because I've knocked on the door and Jesus opened it for me! Thank you, Father, for the truth your Son came to bring us and for the life I have because He lives in me! I rejoice that Jesus is THE way, THE truth and THE life! Thank you, Father! Thank you, Jesus!

Dec. 4 *"...for all have sinned and fall short of the glory of God." Romans 3:23*

Thank you, Father, that your Word tells me ALL have sinned and fall short of the glory of God, because you didn't leave any room for nitpicking about whether anyone was good enough to get into heaven the way they were. I praise you for making it clear that the law can't save us, that good works can't save us, that nothing I do on my own can save me, because all have sinned, including me. Thank you, Father, that you have given me your Word so that I might know what to do about my sins, so I could be restored to you. I love you, Father. Thank you, Jesus, that ALL I did to be spiritually born was to confess that I had sinned, ask God to forgive my sins and ask you to come into my life, and I discovered I was born again!

Dec. 5   *"For the wages of sin is death, but the gift of God is eternal life in Christ Jesus our Lord." Romans 6:23*

Heavenly Father, I praise and thank you for the most precious gift on earth, the gift of salvation! I thank you for showing me that the wages of sin in my life were death – death on this earth because I didn't have your life flowing in me and death to come in the torment of hell. Thank you, Father, for sending your wonderful son Jesus to turn my life around! Thank you for snatching me out of the devil's hands and giving me a new life, filled to overflowing with your blessings! Thank you for the beautiful gift of eternal life in your glorious kingdom through Jesus! Glory!

Dec. 6   *"For God so loved the world that He gave His only begotten Son, that whoever believes in Him should not perish but have everlasting life." John 3:16*

I worship and praise you, Father, because you made the supreme sacrifice by sending your only Son to shed His blood on the cross just for me. Thank you, Father, for loving me so much that you were willing to let your son Jesus die that I might have eternal life. I could never find it in my heart to let my son die for the world, but YOU DID, and I can't thank you enough or praise you enough for doing that. I rejoice that I believe in your

son Jesus, who gave His life that I might die to my sins
and live in you, to your everlasting glory! I praise you,
Father! I praise you, Jesus!

Dec. 7   *"If we confess our sins, He is faithful and just to
forgive us our sins and to cleanse us from all
unrighteousness." I John 1:9*

Father, how I love you for your faithfulness to me!
We have all sinned, and because I have freely
admitted and confessed my sins, I rejoice in the
blessing of your forgiveness. Thank you, Father,
that you have not only forgiven me but you have
cleansed me of all unrighteousness and buried
my sins in the deepest sea, never to be remembered again! Hallelujah, Father, I'm clean! I'm
walking in your light and your endless love because I want to stay clean and because I love
you with all my heart and soul and mind and
strength. Because you are faithful to me, I'm being faithful to you and I'm blessed by the joy of
life I have in you! Glory! How I rejoice that you
always do what your Word says!

Dec. 8   *"Behold, I stand at the door and knock. If anyone
hears My voice and opens the door, I will come in to
him and dine with him, and he with Me." Rev. 3:20*

How I praise you, Jesus, for that day when you knocked
on the door of my heart so loudly I had to open it and let
you in. I thank you, Father, that Jesus said if I heard His
voice He would come into me and dine with me. BE-
CAUSE I HEARD HIM, HE IS LIVING IN MY
HEART RIGHT NOW! Thank you, Father, that I have
the wonderful privilege of dining with Jesus, for I have
never been so fully nourished in my whole life as I am
now. I'm blessed because Jesus lives in me, I live in
Him, and the river of your living water is flowing through
me. Thank you, Jesus, for the marvelous things that
happened when I opened the door to YOU!

Dec. 9 *"For He made Him who knew no sin to be sin for us, that we might become the righteousness of God in Him." II Corinthians 5:21*

Thank you, Father, that Jesus, the sinless, spotless pure Lamb of God, was willing to take all the sin of the world upon His shoulders that I might receive your righteousness in Him. How I love you, Father, that you were willing to let your Son go through such a terrible ordeal for my sake. And how I love you, Jesus, because it didn't matter to you how horrible my sin was, you were willing to bear it on your innocent shoulders and take it to the cross for my salvation. Thank you, Father, thank you, Jesus, for loving me more than I can possibly know in this life. I rejoice and give thanks that because I am dead to sin, I have everlasting life! Thank you for taking my sins, and in exchange filling me up with God's goodness! I received the best end of the bargain, and I love you for it!

Dec. 10 *"...that if you confess with your mouth the Lord Jesus and believe in your heart that God has raised Him from the dead, you will be saved." Romans 10:9*

Father, I confess, I confess, I confess that JESUS CHRIST IS LORD! I believe with all my heart, all my mind, all my strength and all my soul that you raised Him from the dead to show me the way to everlasting life! Because Jesus lives, I live! Father, these words bless my tongue and lips as I confess them, and I thank you and praise you for the love that fills my heart right this minute. Thank you, Father, that I an a new person in Jesus Christ, and because I have believed, I AM SAVED! Hallelujah!

Dec. 11 *"For whoever calls upon the name of the Lord shall be saved." Romans 10:13*

JESUS, JESUS, JESUS! Heavenly Father, how I love to call upon the blessed name of Jesus, for I know that because I have called upon the name of your Son, I am saved! Thank you that I am saved from darkness and called into your marvelous light so that I might know the truth which is in Jesus Christ and be free at last! I praise you that now I have ears that hear your truth and eyes that see your truth, and because Jesus is the way, the truth and the life, I rejoice in the life you have given me. Thank you, Father, for choosing me to be in your kingdom. I praise you that you are Light, and there is no darkness in you at all!

Dec. 12 *"For the Son of Man has come to seek and to save that which was lost." Luke 19:10*

How I love you, Father, that I didn't have to worry and ponder about how to find Jesus and get His attention, because you love me so much that you sent Him to find me! I was a lost sheep and even though Jesus had many sheep with Him in His flock, I thank you that He came to rescue me, personally! Jesus knew exactly where to look for me, because there was no way for me to escape the darkness and confusion of any sin on my own. Because I'm found and saved, I'm blessed in your love! Glory! I'm lifting my loved ones up to you who are not yet saved, and I thank you that Jesus hasn't stopped seeking and saving the lost, and because of your promises, I rejoice safe and secure in the knowledge that as for me and my house, we will all be saved!

Dec. 13 *"Therefore, if anyone is in Christ, he is a new creation; old things have passed away; behold, all things have become new." II Corinthians 5:17*

Father, how I bless you that I am engrafted into Jesus Christ, that I am connected directly into Him, locked in, fastened, attached and joined to Him exactly the same way a branch is connected to the vine, because I've been born again! I praise you that I am a brand new person, because the life of Jesus pouring into my life has made me a fresh, new creation. Thank you, Father, that my old moral and spiritual condition is gone, gone, GONE, washed away by the blood of the Lamb, because you loved me so much. I praise you, Father, for giving me the blessing of new life!

Dec. 14   *"For with the heart one believes to righteousness, and with the mouth confession is made to salvation." Romans 10:10*

I believe, Father, with all my heart in your son Jesus, and I rejoice that because Jesus lives in my heart, I am made righteous through Him. Thank you, Father, that your righteousness is much, much more than the justice of this world, for your righteousness is perfect and without error, and because you are a wonderful, loving Father who cares for me, you have brought me into your perfect righteousness. Thank you, Father, for making salvation so simple in your Word, which says that if I believe in my heart and confess with my mouth, I am saved. I thank you and praise you for this big mouth of mine, Father, and I'm telling the whole world I'M SAVED, I'M SAVED, I'M SAVED! Hallelujah!

Dec. 15   *"Who gave (yielded) Himself up [to atone] for our sins (and to save and sanctify us), in order to rescue and deliver us from this present wicked age and world order, in accordance with the will and purpose and plan of our God and Father." Galatians 1:4 Amp.*

Father, I praise and thank you that Jesus was willing to give up His life to save and sanctify me and to deliver me from the sin of this world. Father, as I look around at the sin and corruption so rampant in the world today, I rejoice and thank you for lifting me above all that carnal greed and desire, so that I can be about your business instead of the world's business. It really excites me to know that when you made out my individual plan, you put all the beautiful and wonderful things that you did in my life! I praise you for that!

Dec. 16 *"And you He made alive, who were dead in trespasses and sins, in which you once walked according to the course of this world, according to the prince of the power of the air, the spirit who now works in the sons of disobedience." Ephesians 2:1,2*

Father, how could you have ever loved me when I was dead in the graveyard of sin? I walked in those paths habitually, and yet you loved me enough to stop me from following the fashion of this world, under the temptations and pull of this present day, when I was following the prince of the power of the air. I was under the very control of the devil himself, but you grabbed me right out of the devil's hands and claimed me for your very own! How I praise you that even though I was once rebellious and unbelieving and went against your purposes, that you quickened my spirit! Father, I'll never be able to praise you enough!

Dec. 17 *"...being justified freely by His grace through the redemption that is in Christ Jesus, whom God set forth to be a propitiation by His blood, through faith, to demonstrate His righteousness, because in His forbearance God had passed over the sins that were previously committed." Romans 3:24,25*

Father, I fell so short of being an ideal person in your sight, and yet you declared me not guilty! I praise and thank you for your unmerited favor and mercy which you freely and graciously gave to me. I thank you for the cleansing and life-giving sacrifice of the blood of your Son Jesus to save us from the stroke of your judgment! How I bless you for passing right over all the things I did and ignoring them through forgiveness to give me eternal life! I shall praise you forever and forever!

Dec. 18 *"For we are His workmanship, created in Christ Jesus for good works, which God prepared beforehand that we should walk in them." Ephesians 2:10*

Father, I certainly wasn't any credit to you before I was saved, and certainly didn't look like your handiwork. But how I praise you that I was created by you and born again in Jesus Christ! It really doesn't matter what I look like to the world, because I'm doing the job that you have always planned for me to do. Thank you, Father, that I am walking in your ways and living the good life according to the plan you had put into effect for me the moment I was born. Glory, Father, you've given me my own special path in life! It's mine, it's mine, it's mine, and no one else can walk it except me! Hallelujah!

Dec. 19 *"And all of us, as with unveiled face, [because we] continued to behold (in the Word of God) as in a mirror the glory of the Lord, are constantly being transfigured into His very own image in ever increasing splendor and from one degree of glory to another; (for this comes) from the Lord (Who is) the Spirit." II Cor. 3:18 Amp.*

Father, I praise you for the miracle you did in my life! I love you for transforming my life as I behold the glory of the Lord through your Word, transforming and transfiguring me ever more into your very own image in ways that I don't have to understand, but simply accept. Father, I'm awed and thankful that you are changing me into ever increasing splendor and into increasing degrees of glory through the Spirit, and I rejoice at this mystery because I am being prepared to meet you! Glory!

Dec. 20 *"Nor is there salvation in any other, for there is no other name under heaven given among men by which we must be saved." Acts 4:12*

I rejoice in you, Father, for you understand everything even though I don't. I don't understand computers, I don't understand rockets and space vehicles, and I don't understand how television works. But I do understand and love the simplicity of your Word! How I praise you that I don't have to be a genius to know that there is salvation in no other name except the name of Jesus, and there is no other way I could have been saved except through that wonderful, majestic, powerful and magnificent name of Jesus! Hallelujah!

Dec. 21 *"And Jesus said to them, 'I am the bread of life. He who comes to Me shall never hunger, and he who believes in Me shall never thirst.'" John 6:35*

Heavenly Father, I love bread! I praise you that I will never hunger again because every day I feast spiritually on Jesus Christ, the Bread of Life. I praise you and worship you because there can never be a thirsting in my soul, because I'm drinking at that fountain of living water. Thank you for giving me true food and true drink, for in Jesus I am nourished to receive everlasting life and uplifted to live righteously in this world. Father, I love you for making such wonderful provisions for me.

Dec. 22 *"And having been perfected, He became the author of eternal salvation to all who obey Him." Heb. 5:9*

I thank you and love you, Father, because Jesus is the author and source of eternal salvation for each and every one of us who gives heed to your Word and obeys you. I love you with all my heart, Father, because in spite of the pain you suffered in letting your only begotten Son bear the sins of the whole world to die with His human body on the cross, you did it because you loved me, just as Jesus did it because He loved me. I thank you because even if I'd been the only person in the world, Jesus would still have planned it this way. I love you, Father. I love you, Jesus.

Dec. 23 *"In this the love of God was manifested toward us, that God has sent His only begotten Son into the world, that we might live through Him. In this is love, not that we loved God, but that He loved us and sent His Son to be the propitiation for our sins." I John 4:9,10*

Father, in this world my mind can never understand the greatness of the love that prompted you to send your Son to be crucified, dead and buried until He rose again so that through Him I might live, freed of the burdens of sin, redeemed in His blood and restored to my inheritance of everlasting life in your heavenly kingdom. How I praise you that it was not my love for you, but your love for me that made all this possible. When there was nothing I could do to be raised from death in my sins, you sent your Son to bring me back to life. Father, I bow down before you in adoration and praise!

Dec. 24 *"...Assuredly, I say to you, unless you are converted and become as little children, you will by no means enter the kingdom of heaven." Matthew 18:3*

How I praise you, Father, and glorify your holy name because you don't expect me to be a genius or intellectual giant to figure out salvation for myself, but instead your son Jesus said I must come to you as a little child, with simple, uncomplicated faith. I love you, Father, for the teaching and instruction in your Word that lets me understand exactly what I must do to enter into the kingdom of heaven and abide in your glory. Thank you, Father!

Dec. 25 *"For there is born to you this day in the city of David a Savior, who is Christ the Lord... And suddenly there was with the angel a multitude of the heavenly host praising God and saying: 'Glory to God in the highest, and on earth peace, good will toward men!'" Luke 2:11,13*

Father, today the world celebrates the birth of your son. Saint and sinner alike, we celebrate this day.

We praise you for that Good News which came out of Bethlehem 2,000 years ago, and we praise you for the fact that the same Good News is going out all over the world today touching hearts, and quickening spirits just like it did long ago. Father, today I praise you for my salvation, and I pray for the world. May kings and nations feel your precious Presence on this beautiful day of days!

Dec. 26 *"Do not labor for the food which perishes, but for the food which endures to everlasting life, which the Son of Man will give you, because God the Father has set His seal on Him." John 6:27*

It's the day after Christmas! What a mess! Tinsel that's falling off the tree, wrapping paper torn apart in haste, broken ornaments, sorry toys, left-over turkey. Father, may we not look at the meat which perishes, and the things which pass away, but may we work and seek after the lasting food which continues until eternal life. Yesterday I felt so spiritual, and today I'm so tired, but I praise you that you're just as real, just as special, just as magnificent and just as trustworthy as you were yesterday. I bless you that as I clean up the mess, I can still give thanks and praise to you!

Dec. 27 *"And they sang a new song, saying: 'You are worthy to take the scroll, and to open its seals; for You were slain, and have redeemed us to God by Your blood out of every tribe and tongue and people and nation, and have made us kings and priests to our God; and we shall reign on the earth.'" Revelation 5:9*

Heavenly Father, I offer praise and gratitude for letting me peek into the last days through your Word. Thank you, Father, for letting me know, know, KNOW that my Lord Jesus Christ is worthy to take the book of the seven seals and to open those seals, because He alone was slain and sacrificed, and with

His precious blood He purchased people from every tribe and language and people and nation to serve you. You've made us a royal race of priests to our God, and we shall reign over the entire earth as kings! Father, how I praise you that you included me in, and didn't leave me out of this wonderful world of Your love.

Dec. 28 *"Most assuredly, I say to you, he who hears My word and believes in Him who sent Me has everlasting life, and shall not come into judgment, but has passed from death into life." John 5:24*

My ears are open to your Words, Father! I thank you for what Jesus said, and I hear it loud and clear, because it makes my heart beat with joy to shout out, I BE- LIEVE, I BELIEVE, I BELIEVE! I bless You because I know that since I believe and trust in you and cling to you and rely wholly on you that I now possess eternal life and that I do not come into judgment, and will never incur sentence of judgment, and will not come under condemnation, but I have already passed over out of death into life. I thank you that because I believe in you through Jesus, I have the blessing of eternal, everlast- ing, continual, ceaseless, timeless, infinite, unending, immortal, imperishable, deathless life! Glory!

Dec. 29 *"Jesus said to her, 'I am the resurrection and the life. He who believes in Me, though he may die, he shall live. And whoever lives and believes in Me shall never die. Do you believe this?'" John 11:25,26*

I will never die, I will never die! What a glorious thought! Jesus, you raise the dead and give them life again. I bless you that even though this mortal body shall die like anyone else, the real me shall live and never die. I thank you for that blessed hope. Father, I glorify you for sending Jesus to save me, and I will forever have faith in Him, cleave to Him and rely on Him until my very last mortal breath, when I shall take on immortality and breathe a different kind of breath! I believe, I believe, I BELIEVE!

Dec. 30   *"Jesus said to her, 'Did I not tell you and promise you that if you would believe and rely on Me, you should see the glory of God?'" **John 11:40 Amp.***

I want to see your glory, Father! Jesus, I want to see your glory! I wait with excitement and anticipation for that greatest day when you've promised I shall see the glory! Thank you for equipping me and perfecting me toward that day when I will at last stand before your throne and behold your glory and see you face to face. Father, how I long for that moment when I shall see your wonderful face! I don't even know what to expect glory to look like, but I'm excited thinking about what it will be like to walk into your Presence in heaven for the first time. I'm stimulated and stirred up to see your glory and grace!

Dec. 31   *"No one can come to Me unless the Father who sent Me draws him; and I will raise him up at the last day." **John 6:44***

Father, I praise you for drawing me. As we celebrate the end of another year, I praise you that even though this is the last day of this year, the most important day of all is that "last" day when we will all be raised up to spend eternity in heaven with you and Jesus! Father, I bless you for having blessed me all this year. I bless you and praise you for divine health. I bless you and praise you for your goodness, for your prosperity, for your loving kindness. But most of all, I bless you for the assurance of my salvation!

If you have never asked Jesus into your heart, why don't you stop right now, and say this simple little prayer.

> *Father, I want eternal life. It is the desire of my heart, but I know that I have done things that are not pleasing to you. I have sinned, and I ask your forgiveness. Cleanse*

> *me of all unrighteousness. Jesus, I open*
> *the door to my heart and my life and invite*
> *you to come in. Take control of my entire*
> *life, and make me the kind of person you*
> *want me to be. Now I thank you, Jesus, for*
> *hearing my prayer and for coming into my*
> *heart as you promised. I love you, Jesus!*

Now confess with your mouth these beautiful words: I'M SAVED, I'M SAVED, I'M SAVED!

Printed in the United States
1339400002B/1-81